# EARLY MUSIC SERIES 10

## Play the Viol

# PLAY THE VIOL

The Complete Guide to Playing the
Treble, Tenor, and Bass Viol

ALISON CRUM
WITH
SONIA JACKSON

Oxford   New York
OXFORD UNIVERSITY PRESS

Oxford University Press, Great Clarendon Street, Oxford OX2 6DP
Oxford New York
Athens Auckland Bangkok Bogota Bombay
Buenos Aires Calcutta Cape Town Dar es Salaam
Delhi Florence Hong Kong Istanbul Karachi
Kuala Lumpur Madras Madrid Melbourne
Mexico City Nairobi Paris Singapore
Taipei Tokyo Toronto Warsaw
and associated companies in
Berlin Ibadan

Oxford is a trade mark of Oxford University Press

Published in the United States
by Oxford University Press Inc., New York

© Alison Crum and Sonia Jackson 1989

First publshed 1989
Reprinted 1989
First published in paperback 1992, 1997

All rights reserved. No part of this publication may be reproduced,
stored in a retrieval system, or transmitted, in any form or by any means,
without the prior permission in writing of Oxford University Press.

This book is sold subject to the condition that it shall not, by way
of trade or otherwise, be lent, re-sold, hired out or otherwise circulated
without the publisher's prior consent in any form of binding or cover
other than that in which it is published and without a similar condition
including this condition being imposed on the subsequent purchaser

British Library Cataloguing in Publication Data
Crum, Alison
Play the viol: the complete guide to
playing the treble, tenor and bass viol.
1. Viol playing. Techniques
I. Title  II. Jackson, Sonia
787'.42
ISBN 0–19–816311–8 (paperback)

Library of Congress Cataloging in Publication Data
Crum, Alison.
Play the viol: the complete guide to playing
the treble, tenor and bass viol.
Alison Crum with Sonia Jackson.
p.    cm.
1. Viol—Instruction and study.  I. Jackson, Sonia.
II. Title.  MT338.C93 1988
787'.42'0712—dc19     88–19508   CIP   MN
ISBN 0–19–816311–8 (paperback)

Printed in Great Britain by
St Edmundsbury Press Ltd, Bury St Edmunds, Suffolk

# Preface

I first started writing this book whilst spending a week in a remote house on the island of Barra in the Outer Hebrides. I had gone there to do a week's intensive practice without the distractions of London life, and it provided an excellent opportunity to write down my thoughts on viol technique. Several of my pupils had previously suggested that I should write a tutor which could serve as a more permanent reminder of all I said during lessons, especially as I was unable to recommend any other books that gave detailed advice. Some time later I spent several months studying the viol in Basle with Jordi Savall. This gave me many further ideas about technique which I incorporated into the rapidly expanding book.

Sonia Jackson, a friend and pupil of long standing, has proved an ideal collaborator, combining her knowledge of my playing and teaching with her own expertise in psychology and writing to help focus and clarify my experience and ideas. Being a keen amateur viol player she has been able to see things from the reader's point of view, and has reminded me of ideas and advice given in the course of teaching that she and her viol-playing friends in Bristol have found particularly useful. Above all her support and encouragement have been indispensable.

My thanks go particularly to my teachers, Wieland Kuijken and Jordi Savall, for their inspiration and instruction, and to Trevor Jones, Anthony Rooley, and Jane Ryan, who gave me so much help when I first started playing. Special thanks are also due to Elizabeth Liddle, for writing the appendix on tuning and drawing the figures, and with whom I spent many hours discussing the finer points of technique. Anthea Johns's help in compiling the music list, bibliography, and discography has been much appreciated, as has the information provided by Brian Jordan for this purpose, and by Sheila Marshall on division extemporization.

Finally, thanks go to all my pupils, past and present, who have taught me so much about teaching, and to the many people who read and commented on various earlier drafts, especially Chris Barstow, Ian Gammie, John Bryan, Jane Francis, Clare Griffel, Sarah Groser, Jenny Hayter, Neil Hansford, Philip Moss, and Maurice Rogers.

Alison Crum

*London*
*1988*

# Acknowledgements

Grateful acknowledgement is made to the following for financial assistance in the preparation of this book: The Wates Foundation, The Leche Trust, Mr Percy Lovell.

# Contents

List of Figures and Tables — ix

List of Exercises — xi

Introduction — 1

1. MAINLY FOR BEGINNERS
   1.1. Preparations — 5
   1.2. Bowing — 12
   1.3. The Left Hand — 18
   1.4. First Pieces — 26
   1.5. Revision Checklist — 42

2. IMPROVING YOUR TECHNIQUE
   2.1. Good Tuning — 44
   2.2. Making a Beautiful Sound — 46
   2.3. More about Bowing — 48
   2.4. More Difficult Fingerings — 66
   2.5. Notation — 76
   2.6. Different Bow Holds — 80

3. EXPLORING THE VIOL REPERTOIRE
   3.1. Varieties of Music for the Viol — 82
   3.2. Consort Music — 82
   3.3. Continuo Playing — 93
   3.4. Divisions and Duets — 97
   3.5. Lyra Viol — 107
   3.6. Sonatas, Arias, and Chamber Music — 112
   3.7. French Suites — 121

4. PRACTISING, ENSEMBLE PLAYING, AND PERFORMING
   4.1. How to Practise — 129
   4.2. Playing in Ensembles and Consorts — 134
   4.3. Performing — 137

5. VIOLS AND BOWS
   5.1. Buying a Viol — 139
   5.2. Viol Maintenance and Adjustment — 144
   5.3. Bows — 150

Appendices
   1. Tuning (by Elizabeth Liddle) 155
   2. Useful Addresses (UK and USA) 165
   3. Published Music for the Viol 166

Bibliography 175
Discography 177
Index 181

# List of Figures and Tables

1. The viol and bow — 6
2. Tunings for the viol — 7
3. Holding the viol — 8
4. Holding the bow — 11
5. The forward stroke — 14
6. The back stroke — 16
7. Left-hand position — 19
8. Placement of the fingers behind the frets — 21
9. Notes in first position — 22
10. Extension on the bass viol — 30
11. Barring — 35
12. Chordal fingering — 35
13. Sound-shapes to practise — 39
14. Movement of the fingers in fast passages — 49
15. The bow stroke when string crossing — 60
16. Hand and bow position for fast string crossing — 65
17. Diatonic fingering on the treble viol — 67
18. Contracted fingering — 67
19. Fingering for the D major chord — 72
20. Clefs used in viol music — 77
21. Holborne, *Image of Melancholly* (facsimile) — 79
22. Bow holds — 80
23. The shape of the first strain of a galliard — 87
24. Simpson, Prelude in D major (facsimile) — 101
25. Playford, *Musick's Recreation on the Viol, Lyra Way,* Almain (facsimile) — 108
26. Ornaments, signs, and terms found in Marais — 125
27. Marais, *Fantasie* from *Troisième livre* (facsimile) — 127
28. Less common viols and their tunings — 140
29. Renaissance viol after Ciciliano (*c.*1560) by Martin Edmunds — 141
30. Seven-string bass viol after Bertrand (1704) by Robert Eyland — 141
31. Treble viol after Jaye (*c.*1630) by Neil Hansford — 142
32. Alto viol after Jaye (1662) by Norman Myall — 142
33. Tenor viol after Rose (1598) by David Rubio — 143
34. Bass viol after Rose (1595) by Robert Eyland — 143
35. Types of string — 146

36. Attaching the string at the tailpiece — 148
37. A correctly wound string — 148
38. The standard fret knot, viewed from behind the neck — 150
39. Types of bow — 151

APPENDIX I

Figures
1. The harmonic series — 155
2. Beating harmonics — 156
3. The Pythagorean comma — 156
4. The syntonic comma — 156
5. Fretting schemes — 159
6. Position of finger in relation to fret — 162

Table 1. Unequal temperaments, deviation from equal temperament, in cents — 160

# List of Exercises

| | |
|---|---:|
| 1. First-position fingering | 23 |
| 2. Fingering in groups | 24 |
| 3. Holding fingers down | 25 |
| 4. Tucking | 27 |
| 5. The notes in half position | 28 |
| 6. The notes in extended position | 29 |
| 7. Extensions | 31 |
| 8. Uneven bowing | 33 |
| 9. Chordal fingerings | 36 |
| 10. Contracted fingerings | 38 |
| 11. Simple string crossings | 40 |
| 12. Tuning method | 45 |
| 13. Fast notes | 50 |
| 14. Co-ordination on one string | 51 |
| 15. Co-ordination in string crossing | 52 |
| 16. Finger and arm movement in dotted notes | 53 |
| 17. Fast and slow dotted notes | 53 |
| 18. When to tuck on dotted notes | 54 |
| 19. Bow direction on dotted notes | 54 |
| 20. Triplet bowing | 55 |
| 21. Dotted notes in triple time | 55 |
| 22. Scales in triplets | 56 |
| 23. Slurring | 56 |
| 24. More difficult slurs | 57 |
| 25. Slurred string crossing | 58 |
| 26. Tucking on fast notes | 59 |
| 27. Legato tucking | 59 |
| 28. Resonance | 61 |
| 29. Octaves | 63 |
| 30. Octaves in semiquavers | 64 |
| 31. String crossings using the hand | 65 |
| 32. Crawling | 67 |
| 33. Alternative routes to the top fret | 69 |
| 34. Double stopping in thirds | 71 |
| 35. Common chords | 72 |

| | | |
|---|---|---|
| 36. | Practising chords | 74 |
| 37. | *In nomine* | 84 |
| 38. | *La Spagna* | 84 |
| 39. | Holborne, *The Funerals* | 86 |
| 40. | Tomkins, Pavan à 5 | 87 |
| 41. | Holborne, *Muy Linda* | 88 |
| 42. | Jenkins, *Coranto* | 89 |
| 43. | Locke, Sarabande from Suite in D | 90 |
| 44. | Handel, Sonata in G minor, Op. 1, Larghetto | 94 |
| 45. | Handel, Sonata in A minor, Op. 1, Allegro | 95 |
| 46. | Purcell, *Music for a while* | 97 |
| 47. | Simpson, Exercise for holding fingers | 99 |
| 48. | Simpson, Chord exercises | 99 |
| 49. | Simpson, Prelude in D major | 100 |
| 50. | Simpson, Divisions in E minor, variation 4 | 102 |
| 51. | Rognoni, Divisions on *Vestiva i colli* | 103 |
| 52. | Anon., *Bergamasca* | 104 |
| 53. | Jenkins, Ground | 105 |
| 54. | Locke, Courante from Suite in D | 107 |
| 55. | Sumarte, *Daphne*, tablature and transcription | 109 |
| 56. | Hume, *I am Falling* | 112 |
| 57. | Telemann, Sonata in A minor, Allegro | 113 |
| 58. | Telemann, Sonata in E minor, Cantabile | 114 |
| 59. | Telemann, Sonata in E minor, Allegro (2nd movement) | 115 |
| 60. | Bach, Sonata in G major, Allegro | 116 |
| 61. | Bach, Sonata in D major, Allegro (4th movement) | 117 |
| 62. | Bach, Sonata in G minor, Vivace | 118 |
| 63. | Abel, Sonata in G major, Adagio | 119 |
| 64. | Abel, Prelude in D minor | 120 |
| 65. | Schenk, Prelude in D minor | 121 |
| 66. | Marais, Menuet from Suite in A minor (*Cinquième livre*) | 126 |
| 67. | Marais, Prelude in G major (*Deuxième livre*) | 127 |
| 68. | Dotted rhythms in Marais | 128 |
| 69. | Marais, *Sonnerie de Ste Geneviève* | 128 |

# Introduction

This book takes you step by step from the very first stages of playing the viol through to the advanced technical level required by the solo music of great composers for the instrument such as Simpson, Marais, and J. S. Bach. The steps are small and should not be hurried, so that if you are starting from the beginning you can enjoy the experience of continuous progress. You may get on faster with a teacher, but the book is addressed equally to those many viol players who have to teach themselves.

The viol has alternated between periods of great popularity and almost complete neglect. For more than two hundred years it rivalled the lute as the most favoured musical instrument, but for the whole of the nineteenth century it was regarded as a curiosity (though the bass viol, as we know from Hardy's *Under the Greenwood Tree*, was still to be found hanging on the walls of English country farmhouses and used to accompany hymns and dancing).

In the great revival of early music started by Arnold Dolmetsch and his family, the viol began to be played again. Performances and recordings by professional viol players helped to create a wider audience for Renaissance and Baroque music played on the instruments for which it was written. And in the last twenty years, with greatly increased accessibility of instruments and music, it has become a practical possibility for more people to play the viol. There are now many viol makers producing high-quality instruments, while at the same time much of the music that had been lying unnoticed in libraries and private collections has been transcribed and published in performing editions.

But there is still the problem of knowing how to start, and some would-be viol players may have been deterred by the lack of a comprehensive, up-to-date tutor. This book attempts to meet that need. It is intended for the enthusiastic amateur as well as the serious student, and recognizes that many readers will have limited time to devote to practice. Those with more time can use the musical exercises as a starting-point for further study. For teachers the many exercises relating to specific technical points can reinforce instruction given in lessons.

No previous knowledge is assumed except that of basic musical notation. However, familiarity with Renaissance and/or Baroque music is an asset, as is experience of singing polyphonic music or playing the recorder. Those who are already competent performers on other instruments can expect to progress faster.

In particular, players of other string instruments will find some aspects of bowing quite similar, and they will already have the required finger dexterity which takes time to develop. But depending on the instrument there can be special problems to overcome too: violinists often find the left-hand position on the viol difficult, and cellists must remember to keep both elbows down.

The viol is ideal for the adult beginner, even those who have never played an instrument before. The fact that it is fretted makes it easier to play in tune in the early stages and much of the best consort music for viols is technically quite straightforward, in contrast to the classical string quartet, which usually remains beyond the technical facility of late starters.

The viol is not generally thought of as a children's instrument, but in sixteenth-century England viol playing was an important element in the education of choirboys, who not only sang services but were regularly employed to perform incidental music for feasts and celebrations. A 1560 account of a Goldsmiths' Company banquet records that 'all ye dinner tyme ye syngyng chyldren of Paules played upon their vialles & songe verye pleasaunt songes to ye delectacion & reioysynge of ye whole companie'. Work in schools has shown what a good introduction to music the viol can be. Both treble and tenor viols are good sizes for children, and they usually find the playing position far more comfortable than that on the violin. This book may help music teachers to offer more young people a chance to play the viol.

The technique described here combines ideas derived from a number of sources: from the many extant seventeenth- and eighteenth-century treatises (see Bibliography), from study and discussion with leading present-day players, from personal performing experience, and from teaching pupils of all ages and standards. However, there are many ways of playing the viol and the approach set out here should be regarded only as a basis, to be adapted to your own individual needs.

Part 1, 'Mainly for Beginners', introduces all the fundamental techniques of viol playing. While this can function as a self-contained unit, ideally it should be used alongside the companion volume of solos, available in treble, tenor, and bass editions (*First Solos for Treble Viol*, *First Solos for Tenor Viol*, and *First Solos for Bass Viol*, selected and edited by Alison Crum). If you are already an experienced player you may still find Part 1 useful as a means of checking that your playing rests on a secure technical foundation, especially if you are self-taught.

Part 2 discusses and illustrates more complex aspects of viol technique (many of which are introduced towards the end of the *First Solos* volumes). All the exercises up to this point are written out for treble, tenor, and bass viols in the appropriate clefs.

Part 3 is a survey of the viol repertoire, which analyses difficulties in particular pieces and demonstrates how these can be overcome. Since most of these works were written for bass, the majority of examples are given in bass clef, but many of them can also be played on other sizes of viol. This part of the book will in general be most relevant to intermediate and advanced players, but the section on consort music will also be of interest to beginners.

In Part 4 the focus shifts to less technical matters. It offers advice on effective practice, on playing with others, and gives some hints on performing in public. Part 5 provides information on buying and looking after viols and bows.

Those who are interested in the finer points of tuning will find them explained by Elizabeth Liddle in Appendix 1. Finally, there are listings of printed music for the viol, a selected bibliography, and recommended recordings.

The soldier and composer Captain Tobias Hume, who took his viol all over Europe on his campaigns, wrote in 1605: 'I protest the Trinitie of Musique, parts, Passion and Division, to be as gracefully united in the Gambo Violl as in the most received Instrument that is.' We believe that this is just as true today, and hope that this book will not only be helpful to existing players but will encourage far more people to play the viol and to discover the great repertoire of music written for it.

# I
# Mainly for Beginners

## 1.1. Preparations

*Acquiring a viol*

The viol and bow are illustrated in Fig. 1. There are many different kinds of viol available, and choosing the one which will suit you best depends on the kind of music you like to play, the people you play with, the size you find physically most comfortable, and the sound that appeals to you. You may not know some of these things until you have been playing for a time, so to begin with it is probably better to borrow a viol than to buy one. Viol players often own more than one instrument, and may be prepared to lend one for a short period; otherwise some organizations, in particular the Viola da Gamba Societies of Great Britain and America, have viols for hire. Once you have played for a little while, you should have a clearer idea about the kind of instrument you want.

Many people start by buying a cheap viol in the belief that it will be adequate for the initial stages. The problem is that it takes a developed technique to get a good sound from a poor instrument, and it can be very frustrating early on to be doing things correctly and still producing a thin, scratchy tone. Badly adjusted bridges and pegs that stick or slip add to the difficulties. If you do buy a viol right at the beginning, take expert advice and buy the very best you can afford. (See Sections 5.1 and 5.3 for more detailed advice on choosing and buying viols and bows.)

*Tuning*

Before you can play your viol you need to tune it. Learning to tune quickly and accurately is an important accomplishment for a viol player. Viol strings are made of gut and are highly sensitive to changes in atmosphere and temperature. As a result, they need to be tuned more often than is the case with 'modern' string instruments, which usually have metal strings.

1.1. Preparations

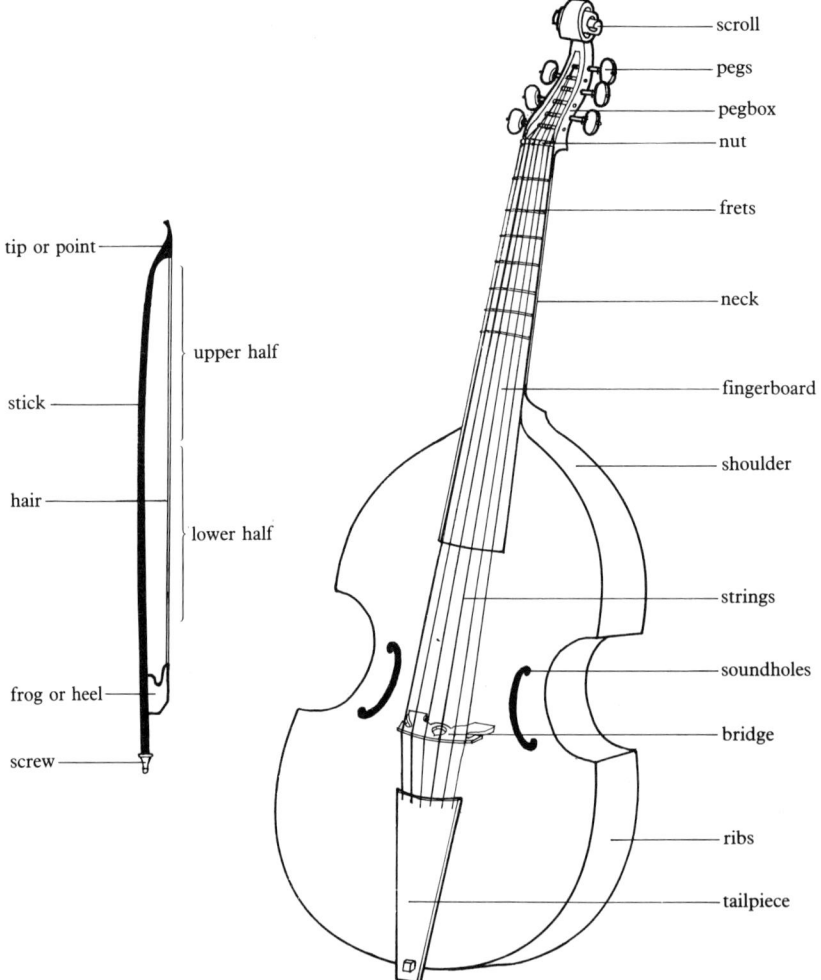

Fig. 1. The viol and bow

If the pegs fit well, you will in time be able to tune with your left hand while you hold the viol in the playing position and bow the strings. But to begin with it is much easier to turn the pegs with the viol facing you, either resting on the ground or on your knee, depending on the size of the instrument.

The tunings for treble, tenor, and bass viols are shown in Fig. 2. In every case, the top and bottom strings are tuned to the same note, two octaves apart. The interval between adjacent strings is a fourth, except between the middle two, where it is a major third. In time your ear will become accustomed to these intervals so that you can tune the whole viol from a single note. Until then, if you have a keyboard instrument or tuning meter, you will probably find it easier to

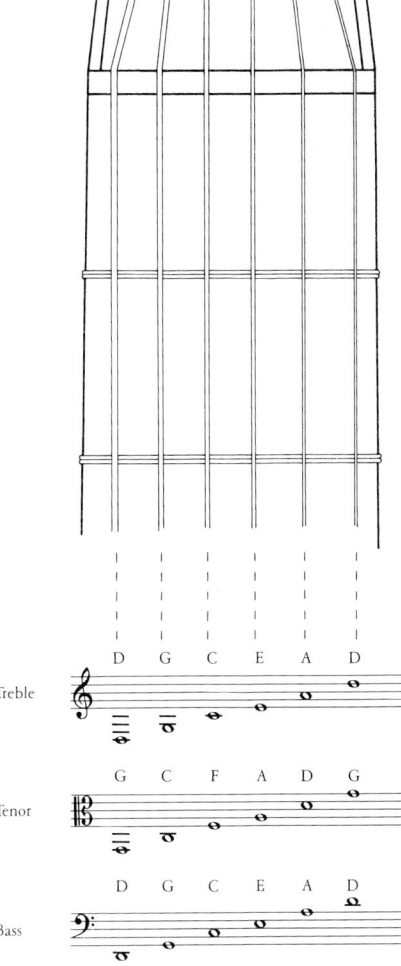

Fig. 2. Tunings for the viol

tune each string to that. A less reliable method is to stop each string at the fifth fret (or fourth fret on the fourth string) to obtain a unison with the string above. Further advice on tuning is given in Sections 2.1, 3.2, and Appendix 1.

## Holding the viol

'The first point to observe when placing the viol in position', says Rousseau (1687), 'is to take a comfortable chair which is neither too high nor too low' and, adds Loulié (1700), 'never an armchair'.

You need to find a position that will enable you to bow all the strings freely. Experiment with different chairs until you find the most comfortable one for

# 1.1. Preparations

viol playing and then try to use it regularly. The chair should be firm and flat. Hollow-seated or backward-tilting chairs can cut off circulation and cause backache.

Sit on the front edge of the chair with your feet apart and a little out-turned, the left foot just ahead of the right and your heels firmly on the floor. Turn the front of the viol slightly to the right and lower the instrument until it rests on the calves (for basses and large tenors) or between the knees (for trebles and small tenors). The bridge of the viol should be higher than the level of the knees. You will soon discover if you are holding the viol too low because the bow will hit your knee when you play the highest string.

Next, making sure that you are sitting 'in a comely, upright and natural posture' (Mace 1676), tilt the neck of the viol a little to the left and slightly towards the shoulder until you can just see the bottom three or four strings without leaning forward. The viol should be in contact only with the legs, not resting against the shoulder. There is no need to grip the instrument too firmly; its own weight is sufficient to keep it in place (Fig. 3).

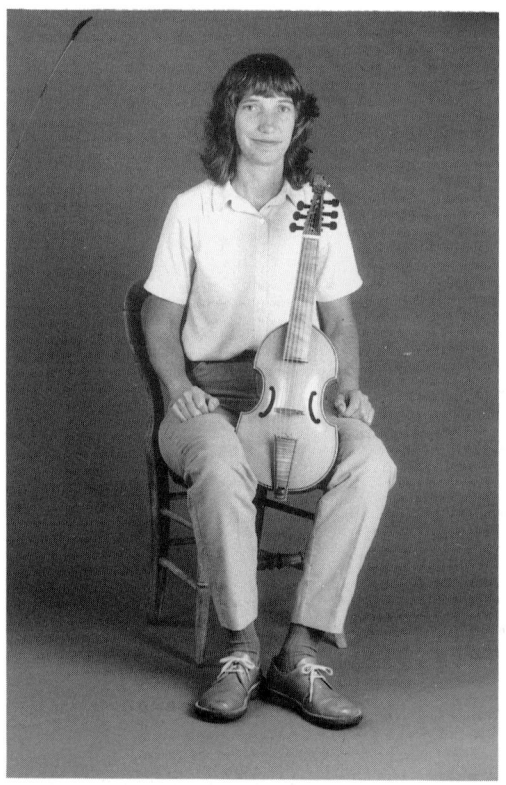
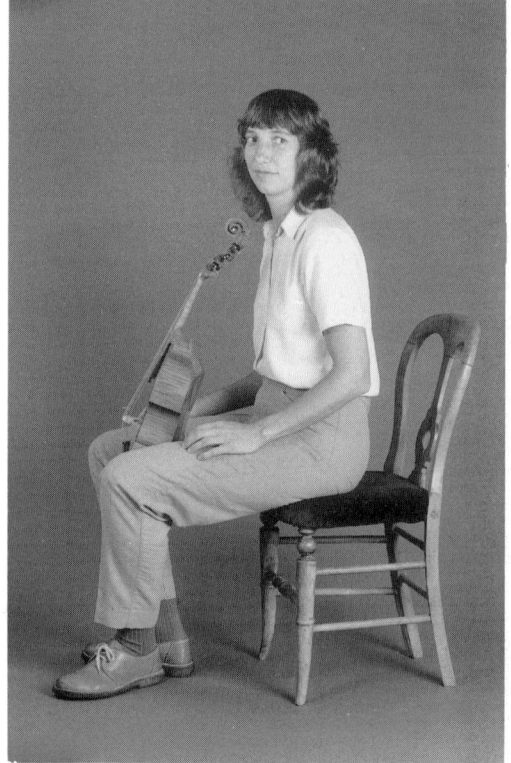

Fig. 3. Holding the viol: Treble

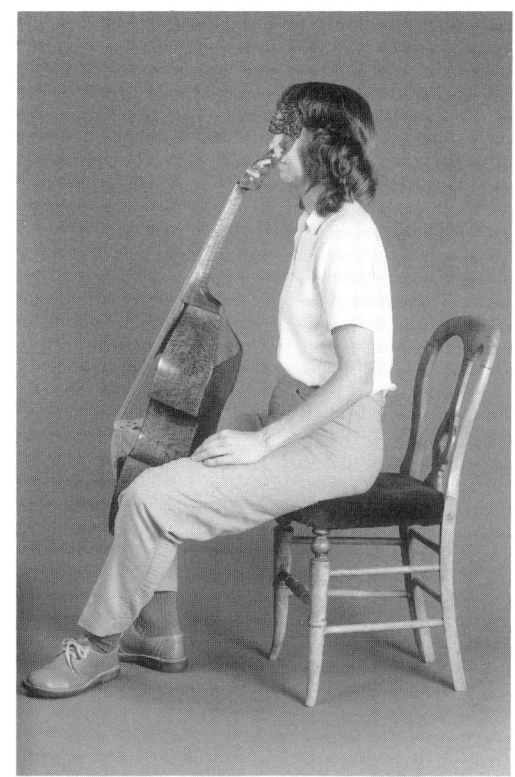

Tenor

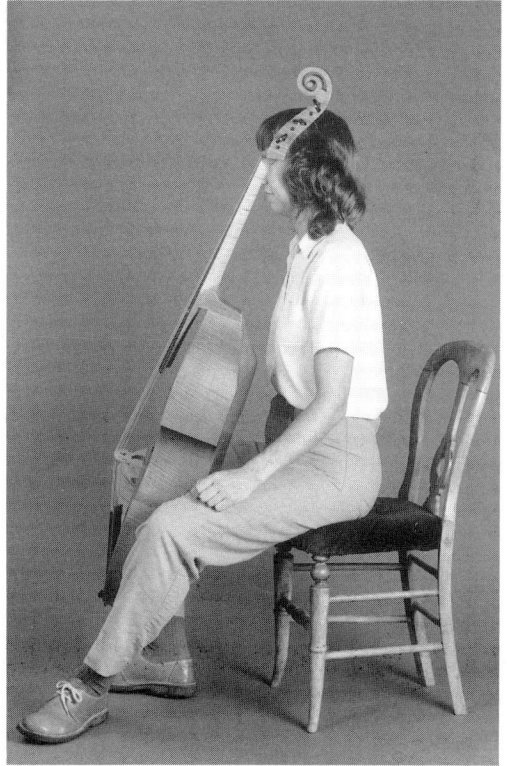

Bass

Beginners often find this position quite a strain, and may even find their legs shaking. This is partly due to using unaccustomed muscles but can also mean that the player is squeezing too hard with the knees or allowing the heels to rise from the floor.

Women bass players will find they need to wear full skirts or trousers. Some types of material, especially wool and synthetics, are slippery and make it hard to hold the viol. A piece of chamois leather over the knees will solve this problem in the early stages and usually becomes unnecessary once the player is used to holding the instrument.

Pick the viol up and put it down again a few times until you begin to get used to the playing position. When starting to play, it is essential to concentrate on one thing at a time. Either practise bowing open strings or plucking the finger exercises, but not bowing and fingering both together. When you get tired of one, change to the other for a while. It is best to start with the bow because this is largely what determines the tone quality. Beginners tend to be preoccupied with fingering, but however fluent a player you become, the importance of a beautiful sound is paramount.

## Holding the bow

First tighten the hair of the bow by turning the screw at the end in a clockwise direction. The bow is tight enough when the stick is fairly straight or curved slightly outward (depending on the bow) and the hair does not touch the wood if you press the middle of it firmly. Having tightened the bow, apply rosin to the hair from the tip to about 15 cm from the frog. (See Section 5.3 for more about bows and rosin.)

Hold the middle of the bow in the left hand with the hair facing towards you and the frog on the right. Extend the right hand with the fingers straight, the palm of the hand facing to the left, and the thumb level with the index finger. Rest the bow on the index finger, about 3–4 cm from the frog. The index finger should be at right angles to the stick, with the hair resting on the crease at the base of the finger. Place the tip of the thumb on the stick, next to the index finger, being careful not to bend the wrist inwards (unless your thumb is so short that it cannot otherwise touch the stick) (Fig. 4*a*). Bend the middle finger under the stick and place the tip firmly on the upper edge of the hair, close to the thumb (Fig. 4*b*).

You should be able to feel that you can pull the hair down towards the floor with the middle finger without the finger slipping off. Keep firm contact between the hair and the base of the index finger. Contact will be stronger if you

*1.1. Preparations* 11

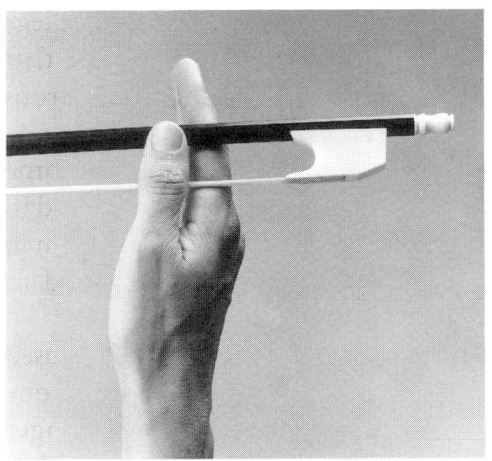
4*a*. resting the bow on the hand

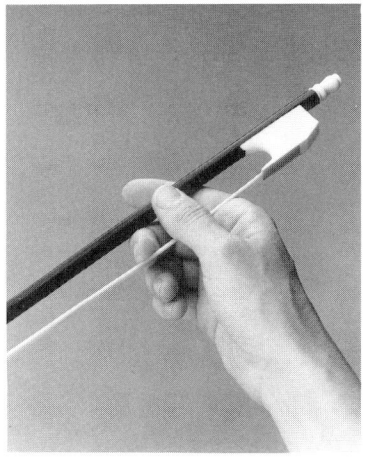
4*b*. placing the middle finger on the hair

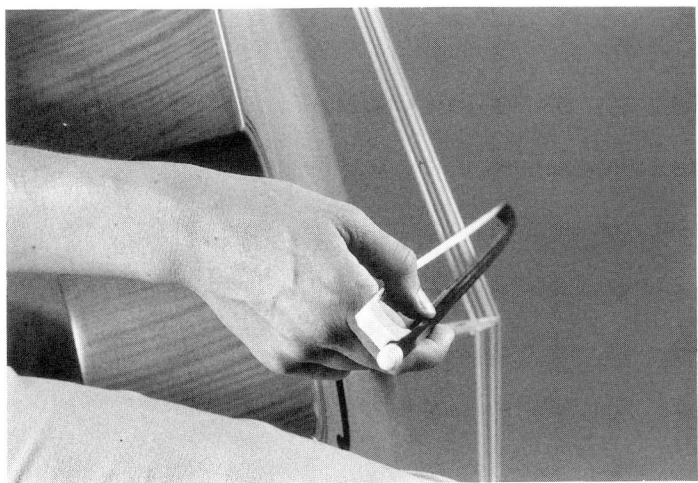
4*c*. dropping the hand

Fig. 4. Holding the bow

keep the palm of the hand close to the original (vertical) position when placing the middle finger rather than allowing it to face up towards you.

Finally, tilt the stick towards the floor by dropping the hand, so that the lower edge of the bow hair will be used rather than the full width, and rest the tip of the index finger on the stick where it feels comfortable (Fig. 4*c*). Imagine that the wrist is suspended from the ceiling by an invisible string, and the hand, elbow, and arm all hang limply from the wrist like a puppet. If you are holding the bow correctly and resting the tip on the string, you should now be able to lift off the thumb and straighten the index finger, so that you are only holding the hair between the two fingers, with the stick resting lightly on the next joint of the index finger. Now put the finger and thumb back on to the stick, but do not grip too hard.

## 1.2. Bowing

*Principles of bowing*

The clear, resonant sound characteristic of a well-played viol is produced by a combination of variable factors, among them the degree of contact between hair and string, the speed of the bow, and its distance from the bridge.

The way in which these factors combine is discussed more fully in Section 2.2, but you should begin by playing one of the middle strings by pushing the bow backwards and forwards and experimenting with the sound.

The degree of contact between the hair and string is determined by the amount of arm weight used and the amount of tension applied to the bow hair by the hand. To make use of the full weight of the arm, try the following exercise. Rest the bow on one of the middle strings, holding the tip firmly with the left hand. Allow the bowing arm to relax completely so that its weight pulls the bow down heavily, squashing the hair and stick on to the string. If you then let go of the left hand, the bowing arm should fall freely on to your leg, leaving the bow resting on the lower strings. Now rock the bow back to the middle strings by pushing down on the tip with the left hand in a see-saw motion. Next, instead of using the left hand, push up away from the floor with the base of the index finger of the right hand, with a force equal to that being exerted downwards by the middle finger. This will keep the bow on the chosen string but should still allow the arm to feel heavy.

The amount of tension applied to the hair is controlled by the angle of the hand as it holds the bow. The more upturned it is, i.e. the more it faces you, the less tension will be on the index finger. Keeping the palm in a more vertical position (as described in Section 1.1, holding the bow) provides much greater tension. You can vary the position of the hand by rotating the wrist to a greater or lesser degree; anti-clockwise gives more tension, clockwise less.

Practise putting more and less tension on to the string by rotating your wrist, at first without moving the bow along the string and later while playing. Take care not to move your elbow away from your side. With more tension the bow should feel very firm on the string and with less it should feel easier to move. If you lift the tip of the bow away from the string with the left hand, it should spring back on to the string as soon as you let go.

Several of the treatises say 'play three fingers width' from the bridge, but this can only be valid for the average finger width. Experiment on one string, moving nearer and further away until you get a good sound—strong but not too harsh. When playing on other strings you will find that the best sound does not come from the same place on each one. In general, upper strings sound best bowed closer to the bridge and lower ones further away. (Later you will also be able to use distance from the bridge to make dynamic variation and change tone colour.) Distances of 2–3 cm from the bridge for the treble, 3–5 cm for the tenor, and 5–8 cm for the bass are probably about right, but every instrument is different. It is hard to estimate the distance from above; to begin with you will certainly think you are much closer to the bridge than you really are.

## Bow strokes

The stroke starting at the tip is called the forward, push, or *poussez* stroke. In contrast to overhand bowing, this is the stronger stroke. It is normally notated by ∨ above the note or *p* below it (not to be confused with *p* for piano). The stroke starting at the heel is called the back, pull, or *tirez* stroke and is notated by ⊓ or *t*.

In general the stronger notes of a phrase are played with a forward bow and the weaker ones with a back; for example, the first beat of a bar would normally be played with a forward bow and an up-beat with a back bow.

## The forward stroke

Put the tip of the bow on one of the middle strings and hold it firmly with the left hand. Push against the left hand with the bow, allowing the right thumb to bend a little and pushing the right wrist in towards the viol, but not too far (Fig. 5*a*). Make sure that the hand is still dropped down towards the floor. The middle finger and the base of the index finger should both be firmly in contact with the hair.

Removing the left hand, apply enough tension to grip the string (as described above) and then allow the arm to swing towards the body like a pendulum. Try to keep your arm relaxed as it swings (Fig. 5), then lift the bow off the string as your hand nears the side of the viol by supporting the stick on the first joint of the middle finger and pressing down slightly with the thumb.

## 1.2. Bowing

This should produce a very loud, resonant sound if you have done it correctly, and two strings may sound together. If the sound is not loud, you are probably losing contact with the string by allowing tension in the shoulder and upper arm to hold back the weight.

If you consciously relax your shoulder and arm every few minutes, you will hear an immediate improvement in the tone. It may help to think of your arm as a chain hanging between the shoulder and the wrist.

At first there may be a grating sound when you start a note. This is caused by the wrong combination of pressure and bow speed at the beginning of the stroke, so experiment by varying these factors until you achieve the sound you want.

*a.* beginning the forward stroke

*b.* ending the forward stroke

Fig. 5. The forward stroke

Practise this many times, using the left hand to steady the bow at the beginning of the stroke until you can grip the string without it. Make sure that the wrist is always leading from the beginning to the end of the stroke. The hand and the rest of the arm should be passive, just following the wrist.

It is very important that the bow moves parallel to the bridge (Fig. 5b). The tip of the bow will tend to point away from the bridge at the end of the forward stroke, so compensate for this by aiming the tip slightly down towards the floor. Unfortunately it is impossible for you yourself to see if your bow is parallel. Use a mirror to check, or better still ask someone else to advise you. Eventually you will be able to tell from the feel as well as the sound.

Once you like the sound you are making on each string, you can start to play notes of a definite length—for example, a semibreve at a moderate tempo. Most people find it hard at first to play just a single string at a time, but this is unimportant. The essential thing at this stage is to play firmly and confidently, even if a few extraneous noises do creep in. Always start right at the point and lift off before your arm begins to feel cramped.

## The back stroke

Start with the middle of the bow resting on the string and bend the wrist out very slightly (Fig. 6a). Now pull the arm away from the viol, leading with the wrist curved slightly outwards as if it were being pulled by an invisible string, and let the fingers, hand, and elbow follow. You should find that the fingers are slightly less bent than for the forward stroke and the thumb will probably be fairly straight. At the end of the back stroke your hand should still be dropped down, with the lower edge of the hair on the string, and the whole arm should look rather like a ballet dancer's, with no ugly angles (Fig. 6b). Make sure that the elbow does not move ahead of the wrist; keep it by your side until it follows naturally.

Play back strokes on all the strings, starting in the middle of the bow to begin with, and later a little nearer the heel. Again, try at first just to make a clear, warm sound, before moving on to notes of a definite length. When you do play measured notes, try to gauge the speed of the bow so that you finish exactly at the point every time.

The most common fault in playing back strokes is to allow the wrist to drop below the level of the hand by the end of the stroke (Fig. 6c). This causes considerable tension and should be carefully checked on every stroke. Also, the bow may slip up too far into the hand, beyond the crease at the base of the index finger. Keep putting the hair back to the correct place whenever this happens.

*a.* beginning the back stroke

*b.* ending the back stroke

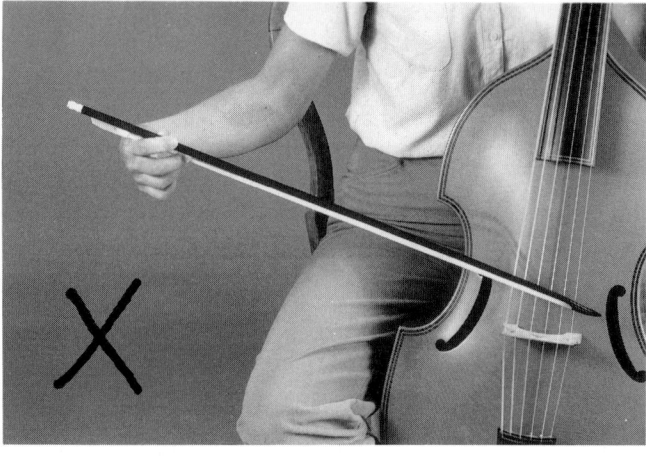

*c.* incorrect end of back stroke

Fig. 6. The back stroke

## Changing the bow stroke

When you are quite familiar with the difference between the two strokes, try alternating them. Begin by having a long rest between each stroke while you prepare the next, but leaving the bow resting gently on the string between strokes. Gradually shorten the rest between each note. Remember that each stroke is led by the wrist, with the hand, fingers, and elbow following. It is also the wrist that makes the change of direction.

To change from the back to the forward stroke, stop the bow at the tip with your wrist curved slightly out and your hand dropped down. Now push the wrist into the normal starting position for the forward stroke; if you are gripping the string properly as you do this, the bow should not move at all. Be careful only to move your wrist; if you move your fingers, the bow will also move, spoiling the end of the note you have just played.

The change from forward to back stroke is harder to manage smoothly. To begin with it is better not to get too close to the heel but to stick to the top half of the bow.

Eventually you will be able to change direction without stopping between strokes. A common fault at this stage is to change the wrist position fractionally too soon or too late. If this happens, go back to the previous stage, with a stop at the end of each stroke. After a time, though, the separate wrist and bow movements will become one action without your having to think about it. Try to avoid jerking or flicking the wrist at the end of the stroke, so that the change of direction happens without a jolt. It may help you to imagine a silk scarf being trailed through water.

Changing the bow smoothly is one of the most difficult techniques to master. The optimistic Mace says 'ingenuity and practise will get it in one quarter of an hour', but you may find it takes a little longer. The best way to practise bowing is step by step, as follows:

1. Loud, 'uncontrolled' forward strokes, allowing the arm to swing freely to your side. Concentrate on relaxing your shoulder and upper arm. More than one string may sound.
2. 'Controlled' forward strokes, one string at a time, of a determined length, lifting off at the end of the stroke.
3. The same, resting the bow on the string at the end of the stroke. Try to avoid an abrupt end by finishing with as little pressure as possible.
4. Loud, 'uncontrolled' back strokes, keeping the arm relaxed and lifting off at the end of the stroke.

5. 'Controlled' back strokes in measured time, lifting off.
6. The same, resting on the string at the end of the stroke.
7. Alternate back and forward strokes, with four beats rest between each, keeping the bow on the string.
8. The same with two beats rest in between.
9. The same with a one-beat gap.
10. Continuous back and forward strokes, starting with half bows and gradually increasing the length of stroke.

Experiment further with different qualities of sound by varying the speed and pressure of your bow stroke. To begin a note cleanly, make sure that your bow is always in contact with the string before you move; do not attempt to start from the air, like a plane coming in to land.

As you practise the different strokes, look at your bowing hand, the position of the wrist, and the hair of the bow where it touches the string. To judge the quality of the tone it may sometimes help to listen with your eyes closed so that you can concentrate entirely on the sound.

# 1.3. The Left Hand

*Left-hand position*

Raise your left hand towards the neck of the viol as if the hand were suspended from the wrist. Keep the palm of your hand slightly turned towards you, with the shoulder relaxed and the elbow hanging down. Place your thumb opposite the second (middle) finger and lightly grip the fingerboard on the third string just behind the third fret, that is on the side nearest the nut. Your thumb should rest gently no more than half-way across the neck and the second finger should be arched and parallel to the frets. Place the third (ring) and fourth (little) fingers behind the fourth and fifth frets, and finally the first (index) finger behind the second fret. For reference, this can be called 'first' position, indicating that the first finger is a whole tone above the open string (Fig. 7).

An alternative way of getting a good left-hand position is as follows. Hold out the left hand, palm down, with fingers spread out as if playing a chord on a keyboard. Point the thumb down towards the floor. Now turn the hand over so that the palm faces you, keeping the fingers in the same position. Finally, bring up the hand to the neck of the viol, turning the hand in towards the neck, and put

## 1.3. The Left Hand

7a. treble  7b. tenor

Fig. 7. Left-hand position

all fingers down just behind the frets, with the thumb at the back of the neck. This should give you a perfect hand position.

### Checking your position

Without regular lessons it is easy to slip into bad habits (Fig. 7e), so from time to time run through the following points to make sure that your left-hand position is still correct.

1. Your fingers should be placed behind the frets. Behind in this case means just touching but not overlapping, so that the fret itself, not the finger, stops the string (Fig. 8). The thumb should be near the third fret, and not too far round the neck (refer again to fig. 7d).
2. Your elbow should be hanging down, not raised as in playing the cello, and your wrist should be curved out slightly.
3. Your fingers should be arched, with all joints bent, so that you are using the

7c. bass

7d. placement of thumb on the neck

7e. incorrect left-hand position

Fig. 7. Left-hand position (*cont.*)

## 1.3. The Left Hand

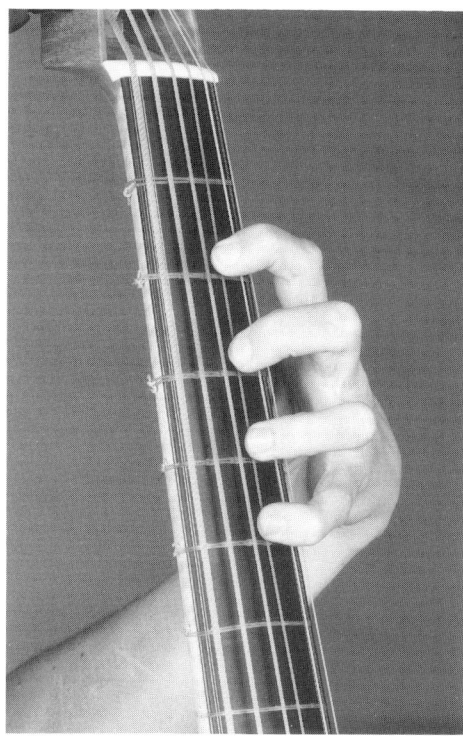

Fig. 8. Placement of the fingers behind the frets

tips to press the strings. The two middle fingers should be more or less parallel to the frets but the outer fingers will curve in towards each other, so you may have to use the edges of those fingers to press with.
4. Press just hard enough to make good contact between fret and string. Try to keep the thumb relaxed. It is very important that the shoulders should also be relaxed and level. Many people have a tendency to hunch them as soon as the notes get difficult.

### *Principles of fingering*

Viol fingers are numbered 1 2 3 4, with 0 indicating an open string. The thumb is not numbered. Fingers should be moved as little as possible. Try to lift them the minimum distance from the string, and always keep them over their respective frets.

One of the most important features of viol sound is resonance, and an essential part of this is the sympathetic vibration of one string with another. The strings will vibrate without being bowed if they are in unison, octaves, or fifths with a note being bowed on another string. Any open note will continue to ring after it

## 1.3. The Left Hand

has been played if the bow is moved away. Similarly, any stopped note will continue to ring if the bow is moved away and the fingers are held in place; for this reason it is most important to get into the habit of holding fingers down whenever possible, right from the very beginning. This is a technique used extensively by lute and guitar players as a means of sustaining the sound.

Fingers should be put down in groups rather than individually. Thus, '4' (i.e. fourth finger) indicates all fingers down, not just the fourth. The first, second, and third fingers should either be on the same string as the fourth or left where they were on previous notes (possibly on different strings).

Where there is a choice, an open string is normally used in preference to a stopped one, except where this would mean changing strings for one note only. Stopped notes may also be used instead of open strings to facilitate runs or slurs, to avoid change of tone colour, or to improve tuning.

### First-position exercises

Practise putting your fingers down as described above. When you are sure your hand is in the correct position and all the fingers are poised over the frets, play Exx. 1–3, first plucking and later with the bow. The notes are shown in Fig. 9.

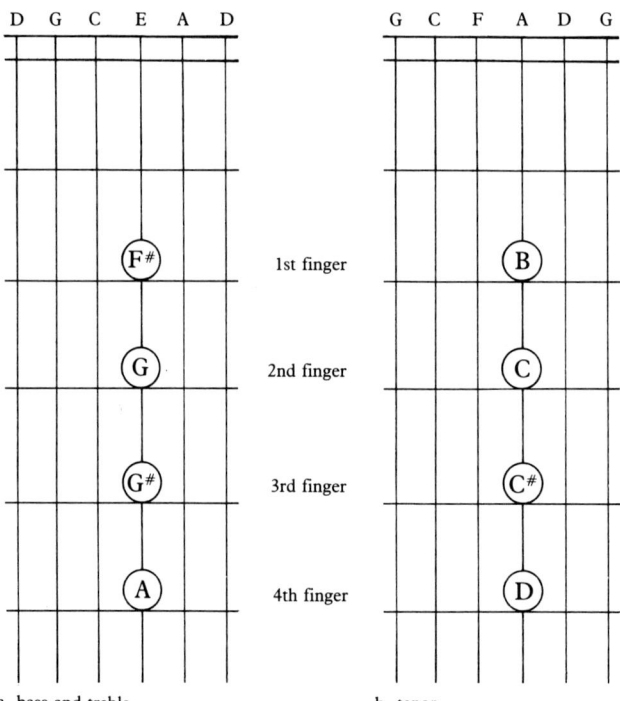

Fig. 9. Notes in first position

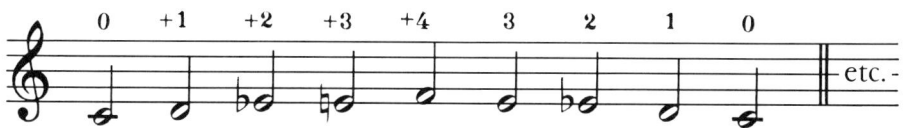

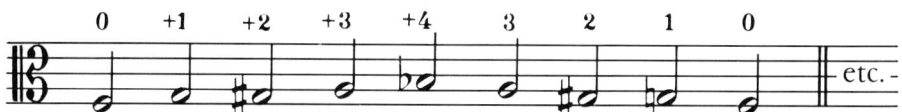
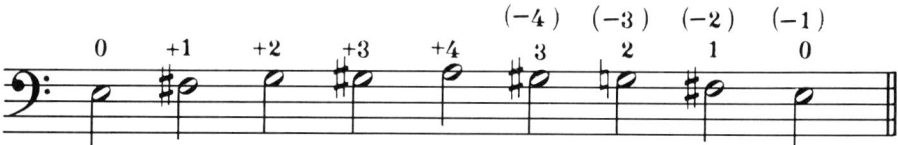
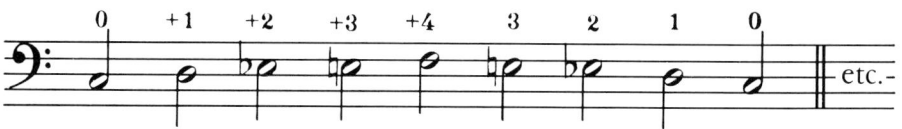

Ex. 1. First-position fingering

## 1.3. The Left Hand

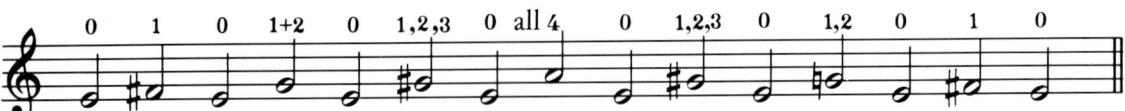

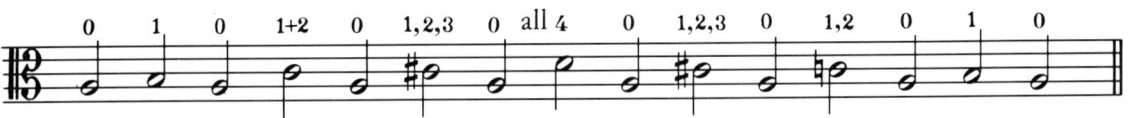

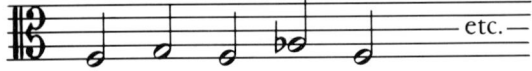

Ex. 2. Fingering in groups

1.3. The Left Hand 25

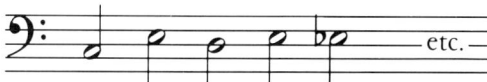

Ex. 3. Holding fingers down

When plucking, rest the right thumb on the side of the fingerboard, a few centimetres from the end, and pluck the string with the index finger, using a sideways as opposed to an upward movement.

The three exercises, written out for the different viol sizes, are designed to help you practise basic fingering technique before you go on to play pieces. In Ex. 1 practise putting each finger down very close to the fret. Keeping each finger down in turn, successively add the next until you have all four fingers down. Then take each one off, raising them only the minimum distance from the string. Avoid pressing hard with the thumb. In Ex. 2 practise putting down and lifting off fingers in groups on each open string. Again, make sure that they are right up to the fret. In Ex. 3 keep your fingers well arched, so that they do not touch the string above. Alternating stopped notes with open notes on the next string up will help you to check this. Hold your fingers down as indicated by the lines.

Practise the exercises on all strings, starting with the middle ones and working outwards. Name the notes aloud as you go up and down each string. If you find this difficult, write out the examples for yourself. For anyone reading from an unfamiliar clef, this will be good practice in associating the note on the page with a particular finger and fret.

## 1.4. First Pieces

Play Pieces 1–10 in *First Solos*; these are all in first position.

In normal first position you cannot play any note at the first fret but in the case of the third string the note at the first fret (F on the treble and bass, B♮ on the tenor) is available on the fourth string at the fifth fret. With this exception you are therefore mainly limited to pieces in the key of G (treble and bass) or C (tenor).

Play as many simple pieces as you can find in this key—for example, elementary violin and recorder music, nursery rhymes, and hymn tunes. This will help you to become familiar with the notes and develop accuracy in placing your fingers behind the frets. Always pluck first, until you feel confident enough to use the bow straight away.

### Tucking

Tucking, or hooking, is used to correct a bowing that has gone the wrong way for the music—when a weak bow comes on a strong note or vice versa. It is rarely used for purely musical effect, as it is in modern string playing.

Tucking involves playing two notes in the same direction of bow without joining the sound. It is always easier on a back bow. Let the bow slow down to a stop in the middle of the stroke, then carry on bowing in the same direction, as if you were making a new bow stroke. Try to release the pressure as you stop at the midpoint so that the sound tapers instead of coming to a sudden, grating halt.

Now play Ex. 4a, practising tucking on back and forward strokes alternately, making a rest between each note. In Ex. 4b gradually make the rests shorter until there is only a tiny gap between notes. Finally (Ex. 4c) practise alternating ordinary bowing with tucks, trying to make them sound the same.

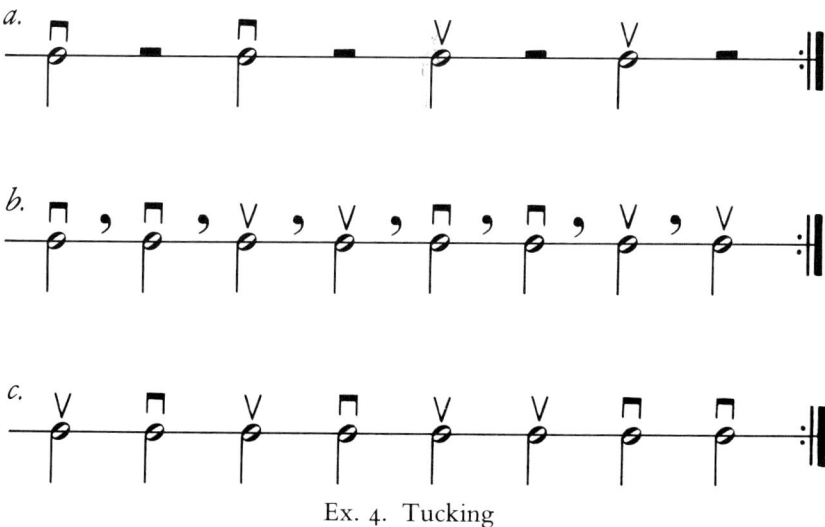

Ex. 4. Tucking

## Half position

Once you are confident about the placing of your fingers in first position, you can extend your range of keys and pieces by learning to play in half position, where the first finger is behind the first fret instead of the second.

Move your hand back one fret towards the peg box and put your thumb just behind the second fret. Your fingers should now be behind frets 1–4. Play Ex. 5, which shows the notes available in half position, and then adapt Exx. 1–3, playing every stopped note a semitone lower than before. Again, name the notes as you play, or write the exercises out at the new pitch and repeat on all strings.

In half position you can play all the notes up to and including F♯ on the top string (B on tenor). Some keys are better suited to playing in half position, particularly when most of the notes are at the first, second, and fourth frets. However, you lose the option of playing notes at the fifth fret instead of using open strings, which means that the bow has to cross strings more often. So, as

## 1.4. First Pieces

Ex. 5. The notes in half position

soon as you can find your way around in both positions (and this is very confusing at first), you will find it best to use a combination.

Play pieces 11–15 in *First Solos*; they work well entirely in half position. Look for simple tunes in the keys of C, F, and D (F, B♭, and G for tenor), and play them in half position.

### Extensions

In many pieces there are only occasional notes at the first fret and it is more convenient to stretch back the first finger without moving the whole hand than to move back to half position. This is called an extension. It gives a whole tone between the first and second fingers, and semitones between the rest. See Ex. 6, where an extension is indicated by a cross between the two fingers concerned as a reminder to stretch a whole tone at that point.

Extensions on the treble viol present few problems, but on larger instruments the following points should be noted:

1. When extending backwards to the first fret it is important to keep the first finger fairly straight, especially on the bass, and to point it back towards the nut, holding the other fingers in their normal positions. This is often quite a difficult stretch, but you will find it becomes easier if you move the elbow down and forwards and allow the wrist to arch more (Fig. 10a). Think of

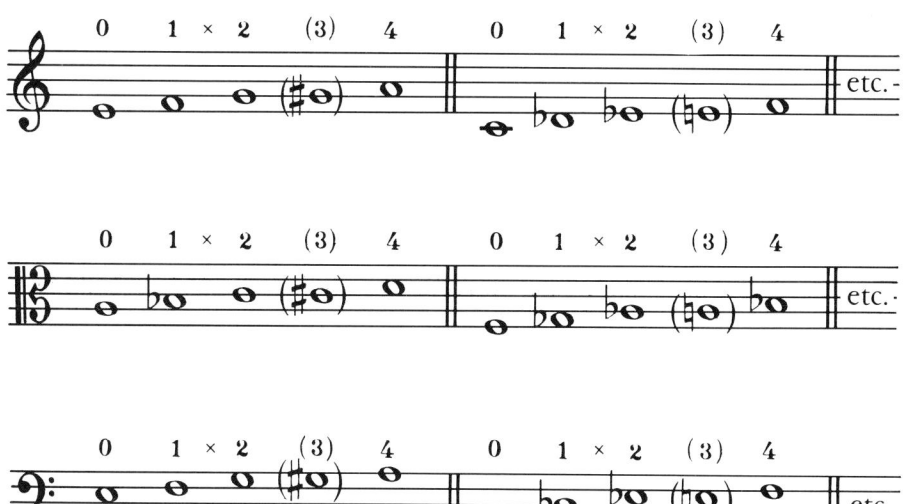

Ex. 6. The notes in extended position

pushing the first finger back towards the nut by making a V-shape between the first and second fingers, and keep the other fingers parallel to the frets as far as possible. Avoid pulling the first finger back by turning the wrist up towards the peg box, as this will cause the other fingers to slope back towards the nut (Fig. 10*b*).

2. Extensions are hardest on the upper strings, so practise at first on the lower ones. On the lower strings the wrist needs to be very highly arched so that there is almost a right angle between the hand and the forearm (Fig. 10*c*).
3. Extensions should be practised first with all fingers kept down, but when the other fingers are lifted they should remain in position over their frets and not be allowed to move back towards the first finger.
4. Extensions between other fingers are rarely used except in certain chords, though they may be used on the treble when a change of position is undesirable (see Section 2.4). When fingering a passage with two whole tones on one string, such as B♭–C–D on the A string, always finger first, second, fourth, rather than attempting to stretch a whole tone between third and fourth. This extended fingering is usually preferable to playing in half position if the passage goes no higher than the note at the fifth fret, since it avoids crossing strings.

Practise Ex. 7 with and without the bow. In Ex. 7*a* put the second finger on the third string at the third fret and hold it there while the first finger on the fourth string moves from second fret to first fret, playing the open string in between.

10*a*. middle string

10*b*. incorrect extension

10*c*. bottom string

Fig. 10. Extension

1.4. First Pieces   31

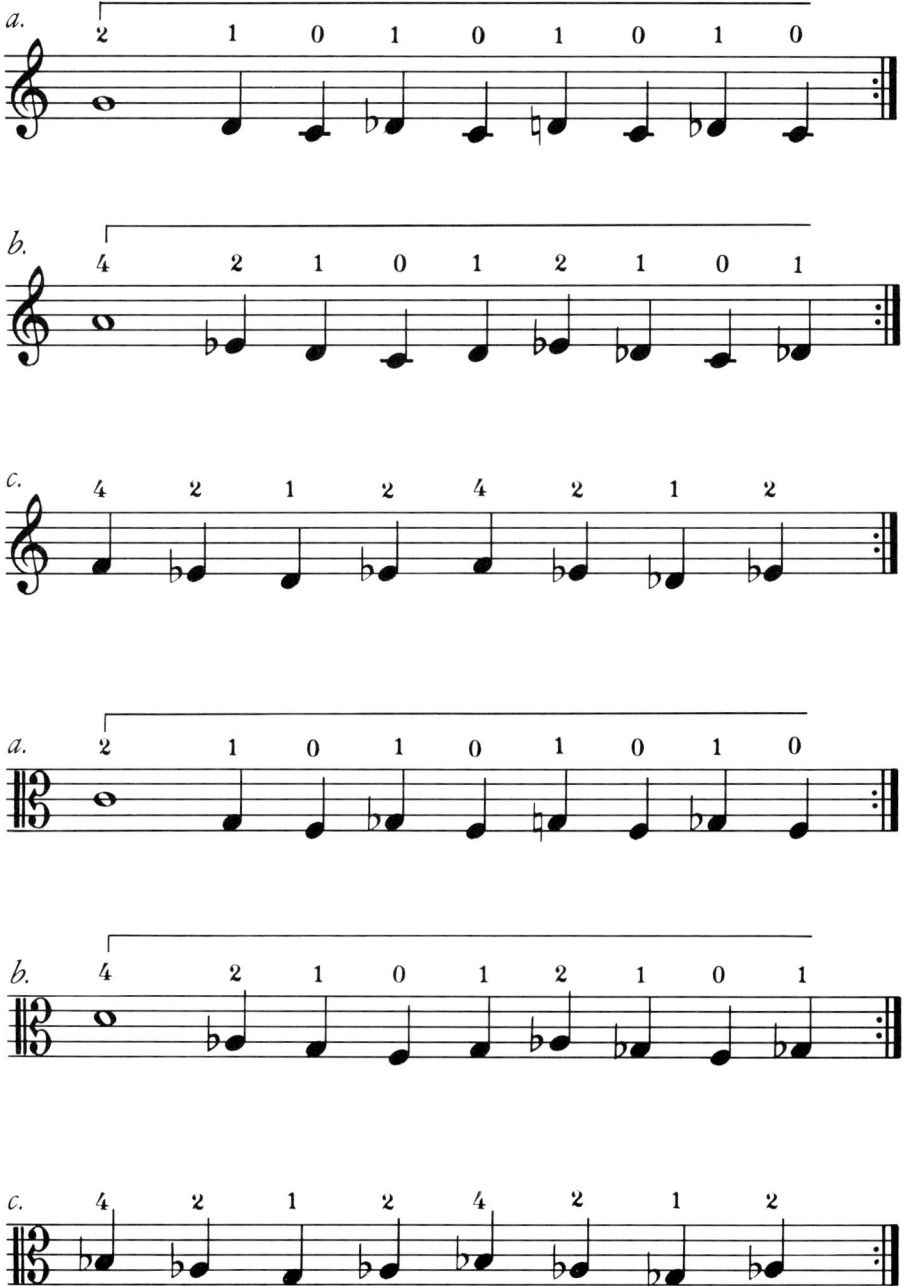

Ex. 7. Extensions

## 1.4. First Pieces

Ex. 7 (cont.)

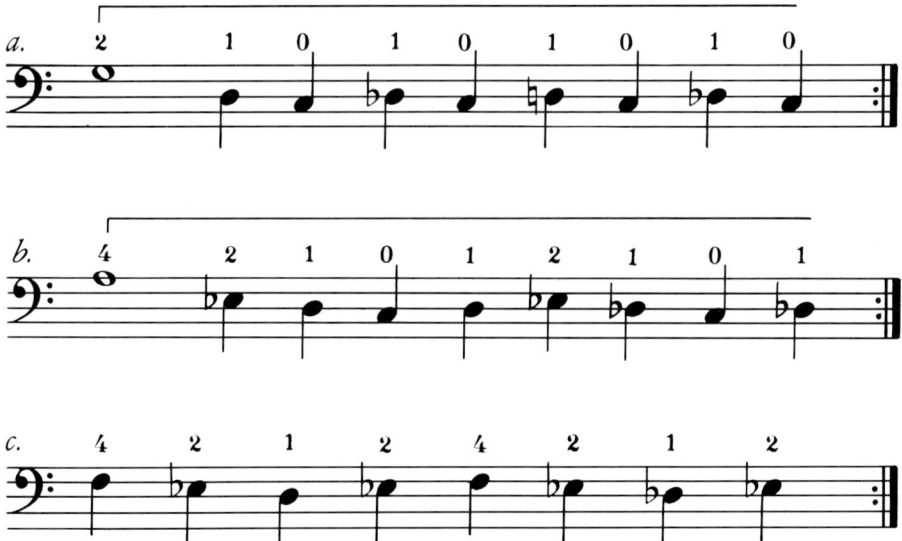

Holding down the second finger should help the hand to stay in the correct (square on) position. In Ex. 7*b* hold the fourth finger down on the third string at the fifth fret and play patterns on the fourth string alternating normal and extended positions. In Ex. 7*c* start with all fingers on the fourth string and play up and down the string between first and fourth fingers, shifting the position of the first finger between first and second frets, but trying to keep the other fingers over their respective frets when lifted off. Finally extend the patterns to include the open string.

Practise all these exercises on other strings (they will probably be more difficult on the upper ones). For further practice, hold the 'spare' finger on a string below the one being played.

Play Piece 15 in *First Solos*; this has alternative fingerings using half or extended positions and shows how a choice is often available. Look for pieces to play which have occasional notes at the first fret and finger them using extensions instead of half position.

You should now begin to combine all three main positions: first, half, and extended, as indicated in *First Solos*, Pieces 16–23. Whenever there are two consecutive notes at first and second frets, for example F to D on the two middle strings (B♭ to G for tenor), you will need two different fingers, that is first and second. Depending on the notes which come before and after, this may be a proper half position or an extension back of two fingers, without the whole hand or thumb being moved.

## Uneven bowing

This becomes necessary in any passage where a longer note is followed by a shorter one or vice versa. If you use the same amount of bow for two beats as for one, the one-beat bow will have to move twice as fast, and will therefore be louder. Since, on the whole, shorter notes tend to be less important, this will sound rather ugly and unmusical.

The first way to overcome this problem, inherent in any bowed instrument, is to make sure that the longer notes come in general on the stronger (forward) bow, and the shorter notes come on the weaker (back) bow. This helps correct the stress, but is still not enough to prevent the shorter notes from standing out. Very often the best way is to use a length of bow directly proportional to the length of the notes. For example, when playing a semibreve followed by a minim, use a whole bow on the semibreve and a half bow on the minim, thus ending in the middle of the bow. In this way the bow speed will be fairly constant and can be chosen according the the type of sound wanted.

Where this type of pattern is repeated several times, as in a triple-time piece where two-beat and one-beat notes alternate, you will very soon run out of bow; in such cases work out how far you can move on each note so that you do not reach the heel of the bow before the end of the passage.

Another way to solve the problem of uneven bowing is to increase pressure and decrease speed on the longer notes—that is, play fairly strongly without using too much bow—and use a very light pressure with faster movement on the shorter notes. In this way, the bow will end in the same place as it started and the problems of travelling down the bow are avoided. In many cases a combination of these two methods is most effective. Pieces 24–8 in *First Solos* provide good examples of uneven bowing.

Practise Ex. 8, which uses the two most common proportions of 'unevenness'. Use a slow heavy forward bow and a faster, lighter back bow. Play each bar many times over, listening hard to see if the short note is weaker than the long

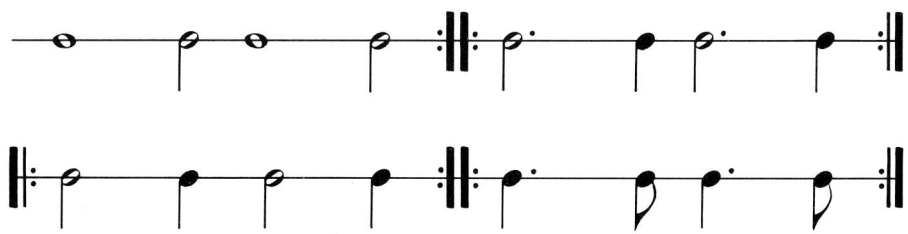

Ex. 8. Uneven bowing

one. The more extreme the unevenness becomes, the greater the necessity to control the forward bow, otherwise you may find yourself with a whole bow to get back to the point in only a semiquaver. Rehearse these patterns with and without travelling down the bow. In a particular musical context, the decision will depend on whether or not there is a convenient place to get back to the point.

## Barring and chordal fingering

Melodic intervals of a fourth occur quite frequently in most pieces, and on the viol this often means playing two consecutive notes at the same fret on different strings, as in *First Solos*, Pieces 5, 6, 12, and 24. Lifting a finger off and moving it across from one string to another makes a break in the sound, and it is therefore impossible to play really smoothly using this type of fingering.

One alternative is to 'bar', that is put a finger flat across two or more strings (Fig. 11). This is very common in lute and guitar playing, but it is difficult to make a good sound on the viol with a flat finger, and it also puts a strain on the hand since it requires much greater pressure to stop the string effectively. The first finger is usually strong enough to cope with this, but barring with the second and third finger should be avoided. They are comparatively weak when flat, and this cramps the entire hand so much that other fingers cannot be used at the same time. The fourth finger can very occasionally be used for barring when no other possibility exists.

When barring with the first finger you will need to use the upper edge of the finger and to pull down quite hard on the higher strings. You may use the second finger on top of the first to help push down if it is not needed for another note. Dropping the elbow may also help (Fig. 11).

Apart from barring at the first or second frets, it is usually better to use two different fingers on the same fret, side by side. This is called chordal or lute-type fingering. To do this comfortably, turn the wrist up towards the peg box a little and put the lower-numbered fingers on the lower strings, for example second finger on the A string and third finger on the D string, both at the same fret, giving C and F at the third fret or C♯ and F♯ at the fourth (Fig. 12). Intervals of a fourth (or a third on the middle strings) are the most common occasions for this type of fingering.

In deciding which pair of fingers to use, choose those which are nearest to the fret in question in half or first position, taking into account which other fingers are needed elsewhere. This means that, at the second fret, first and second fingers are the most likely, unless the first finger is needed at the first fret, in which case second and third fingers are better. Try to keep the hand in the lowest position

1.4. First Pieces    35

Fig. 11. Barring

Fig. 12. Chordal fingering

possible (nearest the nut), and avoid moving the first finger higher than the second fret unless you need to reach a note above the fifth fret.

When using chordal fingering, do not allow your elbow to rise but turn the wrist towards the peg box, only arching it as far as is necessary to bring the fingers into line. Remember that this position is the exception to the rule that the hand should be held at right angles to the fingerboard, so return to the normal hand position as soon as possible.

To allow both the notes to resonate (which is one of the main aims in using these fingerings), it is essential that both fingers are held down. Play Ex. 9.

When playing a rising interval, finger the lower note normally and squash in the next finger on the upper string. On a smaller instrument you may have to put the finger on the lower string very slightly back from the fret to allow room for the upper one. For a descending interval, put down the next finger to the one you would normally use on the upper note, for example 3 instead of 2, so that the normal finger is free to go on to the lower note. Make sure the upper finger is right up to the fret and place the lower one as close as possible. Descending intervals need greater anticipation, or you will find too late that you have put

1.4. First Pieces

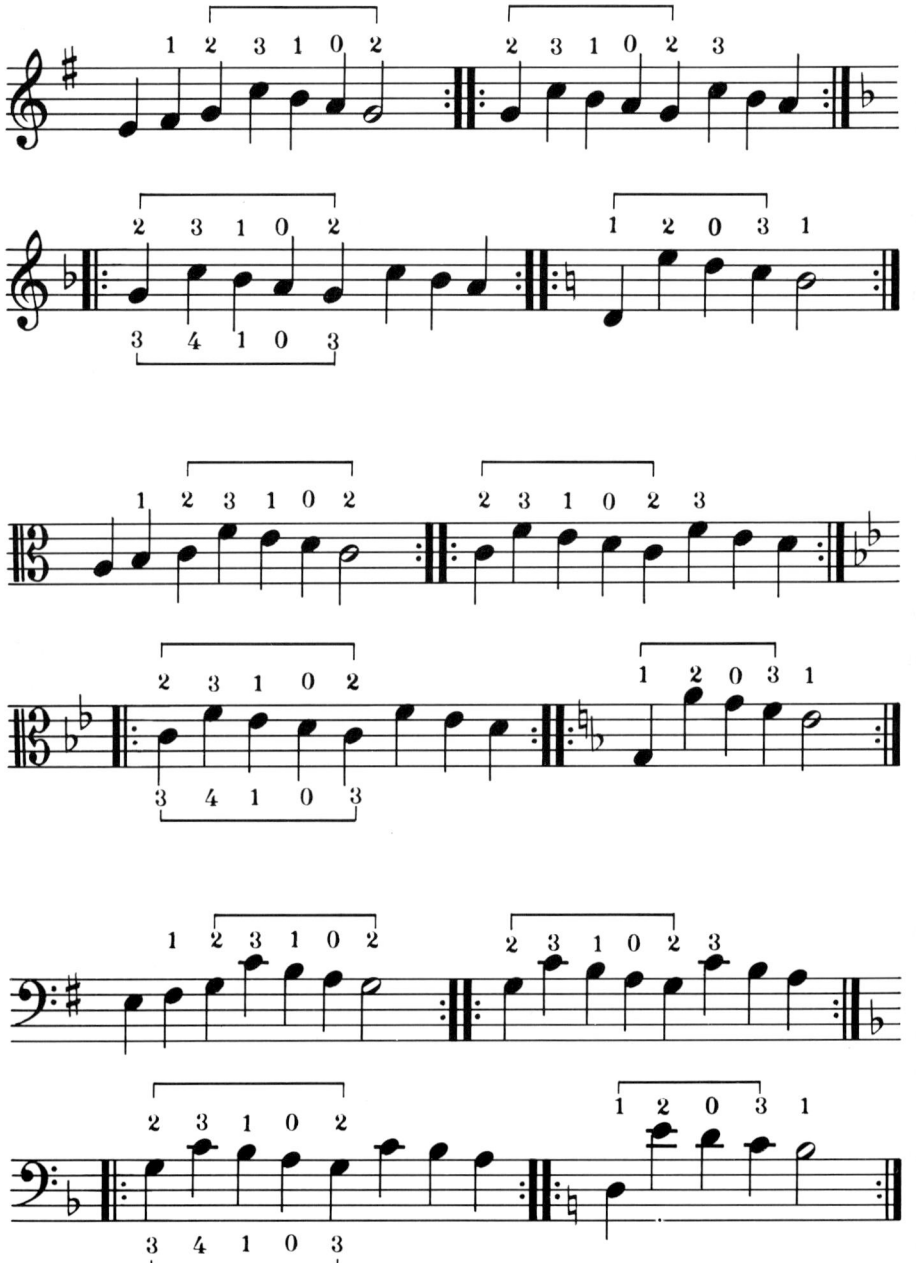

Ex. 9. Chordal fingerings

down a second finger instead of a third and have no alternative but to jump for the next note, leaving an undesirable gap in the sound. Play the whole of Ex. 9 in reverse to give practice in descending intervals. Treble players with large fingers may have to compromise!

In chordal fingerings, first and third fingers frequently lie on adjacent frets. When fingering across a large number of strings, you will find that your stretch is decreased and you may need to use a higher-numbered finger than normal. The same is true when you are barring, because of the cramping of the hand that results.

Try to use chordal fingering whenever you find two consecutive notes at the same fret. Play Pieces 27–31 in *First Solos*, several of which indicate this fingering.

## Contracted fingering

It is often necessary for the fingers to be bunched more closely together than one per fret, for example first finger on B with third on C. As you will have seen, chordal fingerings follow this principle (see Fig. 12). You can use the same type of fingering for moving around the fingerboard, for instance in changing from first to half position and vice versa, or, at a later stage, for moving into higher positions. This is not necessary where there is an open string between changes of position. Practise Ex. 10, remembering that moving smoothly from one finger to another rather than jumping will help to achieve economy of movement and a resonant sound. In Ex. 10*a* close up the hand to bring the fourth finger back on to the fourth fret. While playing that note, move all the other fingers back a fret into half position. Do the opposite going upwards. In Ex. 10*b* bring the third finger back to the third fret, leaving the first finger on the second fret. While holding down the third finger, move the second and first fingers back a fret and on to the lower string. Notice that there is no need to take the third finger off to play the last three notes. Also practise these exercises backwards, reading the notes from right to left.

## Simple string crossings

String crossing, or moving from one string to another, is one of the most difficult aspects of bowing, particularly when the strings are not adjacent. The following points should be noted:

1. Always move the minimum distance between two strings. Begin with the bow already close to the next string up or down, and only move it just far enough to reach that string.

## 1.4. First Pieces

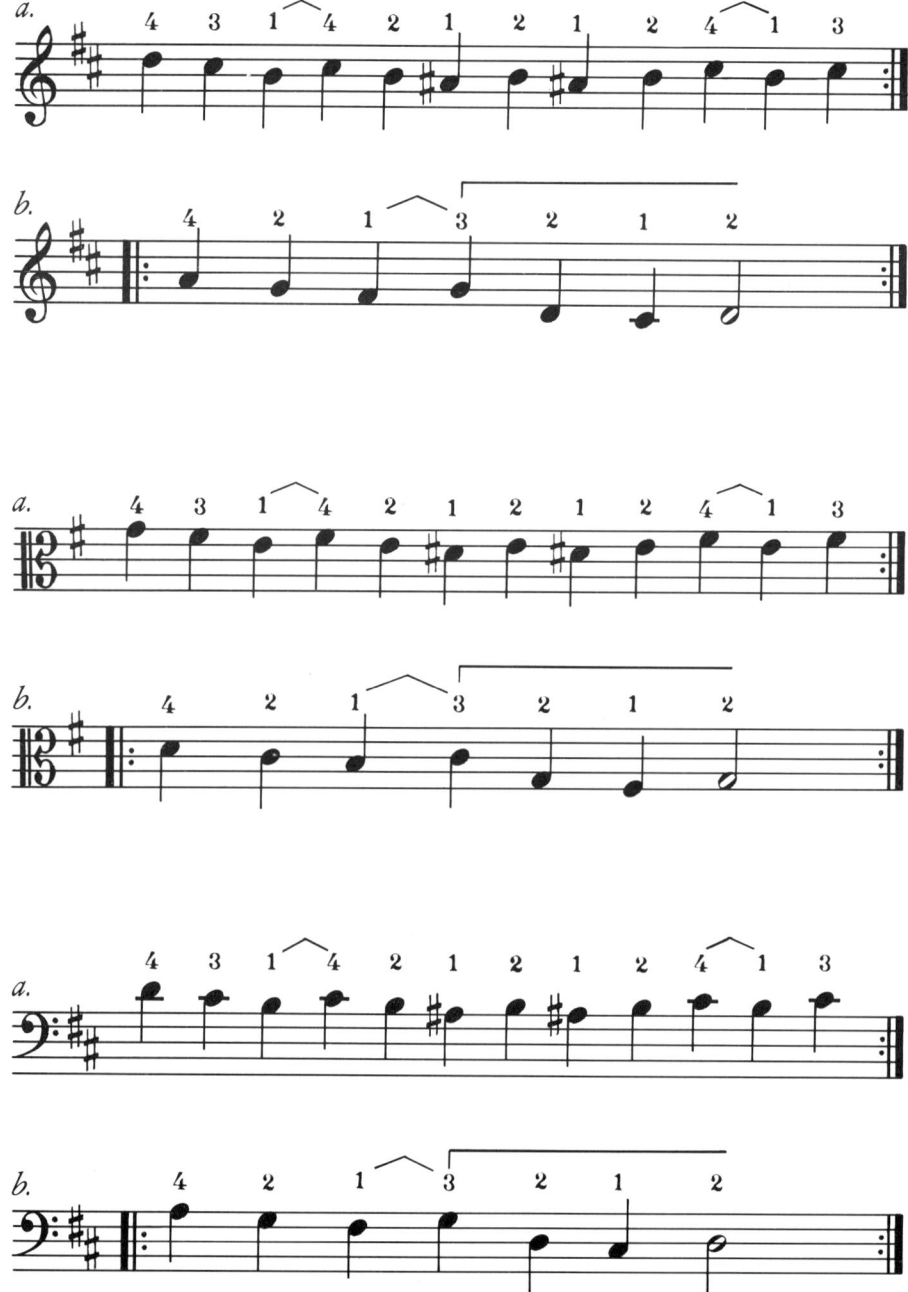

Ex. 10. Contracted fingerings

2. Keep the bowing arm as low as possible. The movement of the arm should be forward, away from you, and back, rather than up and down or around the viol. The elbow should move away from the body in line with the leg.
3. If you have to jump any finger across one or more strings, rather than using two different fingers, always move the bow first, keeping the finger down, and move the finger at the last moment when the bow is ready to play the next string. You may find this quite difficult at first. Practise it in slow motion or with a stop between each movement, as you did when learning to change the bow earlier.

Practise patterns such as those in Ex. 11 on any pair of adjacent strings. Do not be tempted to lift the arm when moving to a higher string, and in crossing to a lower string pull the elbow back behind the body. It is easier to cross up on a forward bow and down on a back bow, but the music often demands that the stress be on the upper note, and you should therefore practise both ways.

## Articulation

Variety of articulation is one of the most important aspects of playing any instrument. Each note has a beginning, a middle, and an end, and you should consider all possible ways of playing these three parts. Beginnings can vary from hardly audible to very accented, depending on the amount of pressure and the speed of the stroke. The middle of a note can increase or decrease in volume at any point within it. The end can fade to nothing, get stronger, or stop dead (though this is not often desirable). When playing any sequence of notes you must consider how one note follows on to the next and the amount of space between them. The most obvious contrast is between very smooth and very detached playing (legato and staccato); between these two extremes are all the intermediate variations and subtleties which you should begin to incorporate into your playing. Fig. 13 shows some of the shapes which notes can take. It may

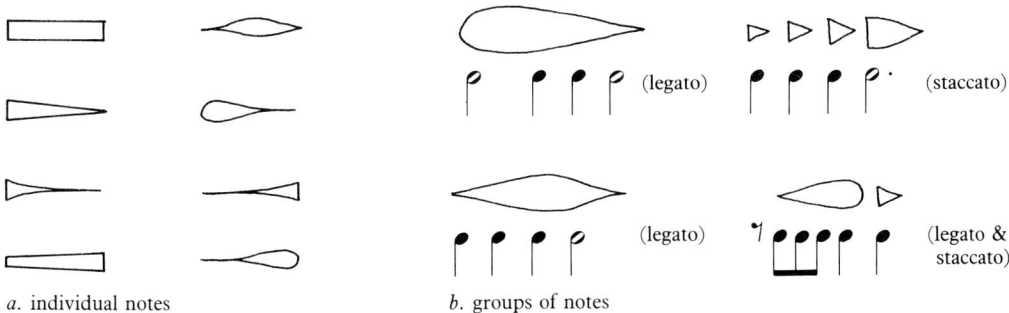

Fig. 13. Sound-shapes to practise

1.4. First Pieces

Ex. 11. Simple string crossings

help to visualize different fruits and vegetables, for example pears, lemons, carrots, and parsnips.

Most phrases that move by step are melodic, and usually sound best played legato. To play any passage really smoothly it is important that you maintain some degree of pressure on the hair all the time, rather than allowing all the tension to be released at the end of each stroke. The natural tendency is to let the sound of each note die away, resulting in a succession of separate events without any clear direction. To combat this and create a sense of line, begin by trying to keep the pressure absolutely constant while changing the bow direction, and then vary the sound by increasing or decreasing pressure, bow speed, and distance from the bridge, according to the demands of the musical phrase. When playing fast runs, there will not be time to vary the sound on each note, but you can still increase or decrease the sound overall.

A more detached style of playing is usually preferable for leaping notes and often for repeated notes at any speed. The viol is rarely played 'off the string' as in modern string technique, but the effect of staccato can be obtained by letting notes die away rapidly. This 'decay' in sound can be effected in three different ways. The easiest way is to lift the bow off the string while it is still moving, allowing the sound to die away naturally as it does on any plucked instrument. This method can be used whenever there is time to put the bow back on the string before the next note, but often this is not the case. A second way is to move the bow across to an adjacent string, allowing the first note to resonate, as described in Section 2.3. In both these methods the decrease in sound is not controlled by the bow, but most often it will be necessary to play in a detached style while keeping the bow on the string. This is done by releasing pressure as you play. To do this, allow the hand to rotate slightly in a clockwise direction. As explained in Section 1.2, this produces less tension on the hair. Experiment with different speeds and amounts of release, depending on how short you want the note to be. To play fast notes detached, stiffen the wrist a little, and make very small arm movements for each note, releasing the pressure immediately on each one. Pieces 29 and 30 in *First Solos* provide a good contrast of mood: the first needs short lively notes, and the second should be played very smoothly. Practise playing the different note shapes shown in Fig. 13.

## 1.5. Revision Checklist

Part 2 introduces more advanced techniques for those who have already been playing for some time. You will have to judge for yourself when you are ready to go on to this stage. People vary a great deal in the speed with which they progress on a new instrument, but this does not necessarily indicate the standard they will eventually reach.

It is most important to make sure that you have mastered the basic techniques before moving on to more advanced music, otherwise the quality of sound will deteriorate. The points below provide a useful summary and checklist:

1. Is your body relaxed? Check shoulders, arms, neck, back, legs, and wrists.
2. Are you holding the hair of the bow rather than the stick; can you lift the thumb without dropping the bow?
3. Is the bowing hand dropped down below the level of the wrist?
4. Is the hair still in the crease at the base of the index finger?
5. Is the middle finger on the hair bent, not stretched out flat along the hair?
6. Is the elbow completely passive, hanging in line between wrist and shoulder?
7. Is the bowing arm in the lowest possible position, even on the upper strings?
8. Are you making a good sound for the beginning, middle, and end of each note?
9. Are you changing the bow direction with the wrist, leaving the fingers behind?
10. Is the bow parallel to the bridge throughout the stroke?
11. Are you close enough to the bridge, especially on the upper strings?
12. Is your left hand at right angles to the neck, with the wrist arched and elbow hanging?
13. Are your fingers right behind the frets?
14. Are you pointing the first finger back when extending, keeping it almost straight?
15. Are you keeping all fingers down as long as possible and avoiding jumps?

Concentrate on a different point each time you play a piece. Eventually you should be aware of all the different aspects together, but at first if you try to think of more than one thing at a time you risk becoming discouraged. Set a small, achievable target and reward yourself with the experience of steady progress. That way you will always want to practise and will soon be able to move on to more demanding music.

Finally, here are some of Loulié's 'Little rules which must be observed in the beginning'.

Feet down flat
The thumb opposite the middle finger
Never lift any finger without need
Do not touch the strings with the wood of the bow
Do not cave the hand in
Do not make a 'donkey's back'
Begin the forward stroke at the tip of the bow
Do not make grimaces
Do not puff

# 2
# Improving Your Technique

## 2.1. Good Tuning

Tuning, often taken for granted, is one of the hardest and most crucial aspects of viol playing. It is well worth spending a good deal of time (and, if necessary, money) to make sure that it is in fact possible to tune your viol properly. The pegs must turn smoothly and the whole instrument needs to be well adjusted. Some advice on how you can achieve this is given in Section 5.2.

It is best to tune while bowing, since the pitch of a note is much clearer when it is bowed than when it is plucked. Use long bows with moderate pressure. As you turn the peg, push it in firmly so that it will stay exactly where you leave it. This makes the peg harder to turn, but, if you wait to push it in until the string is in tune, you will immediately alter the pitch again and end up out of tune again.

For the top three strings you can push the neck of the viol against your head or shoulder as you tune. For the bottom three, bring your left hand round to the near side of the peg box, leaving the little finger on the far side to push against. If the pegs are very stiff you may have to turn the viol to face you, but this should not be necessary if they fit well.

Sometimes you will find a 'notch' on the peg, resulting in a note always just above or just below the one you want. If this happens, try turning the string down about a third and then tune up to the note again. In general, however, you should try to move the pegs as little as possible.

For reasons discussed in more detail in Appendix 1, it is impossible for a viol to be perfectly in tune and there are many different ideas about the best available compromise. Until you are confident about the accuracy of your ear, which will improve rapidly with practice, it is probably best to use an electronic tuning meter, or a well-tuned piano, to check the open strings, and then to check that the frets are correctly placed.

When you come to tune by ear, you will find that you have to adjust the size of the fourths and the third so that the two outer strings will make a good double

2.1. Good Tuning 45

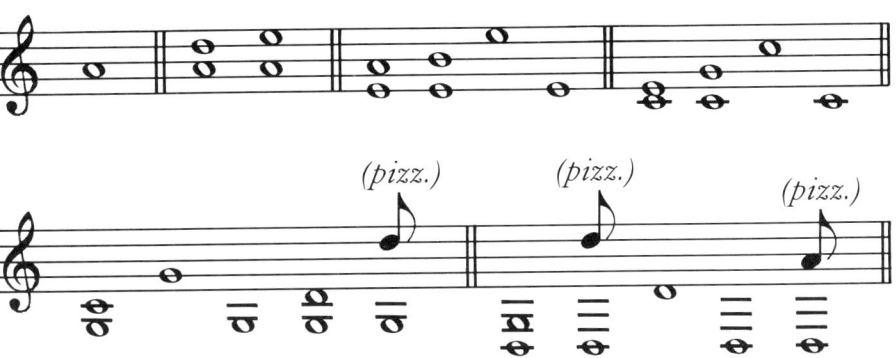

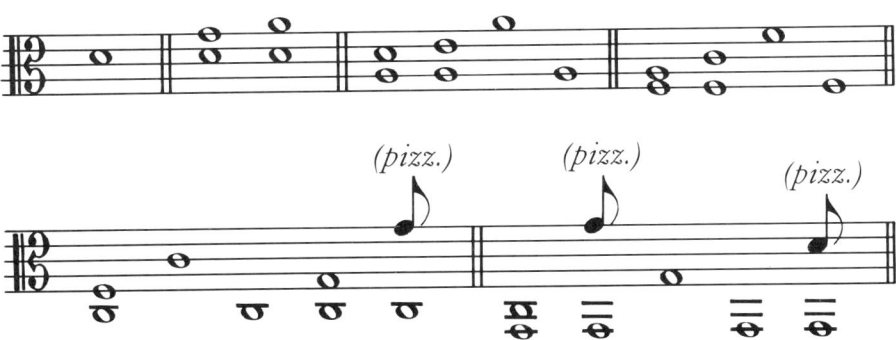

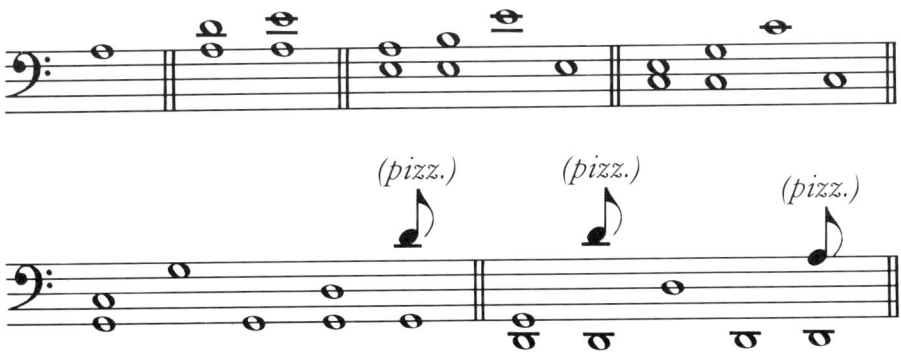

Ex. 12. Tuning method

octave. As you tune the open strings, cross-check by playing fifths and octaves above and below them, as shown in Ex. 12. For example, tune a treble or bass as follows: open A; open D, check E on D string with A below; open E, check B on A string with E below, E on D string with E below; open C, check G on E string with C below, C on A string with C below; open G, check G on E string with G below, D on C string with G below, top D string with open G; bottom D string, check with top D string and D on C string, bottom D string, check with open A string. To tune the lower strings it may help to pluck the open upper strings at the same time. When you think the viol is in tune, play each pair of adjacent strings and listen to the sound of the fourth or third. In this way you will eventually be able to judge when the intervals are right without needing to use the frets. This is desirable because, although you can tune by unisons, matching the open string to the fifth or fourth fret of the string below, this is unreliable unless you are quite certain that your frets are in the right place. Any error in fret placement will be much more marked on the higher-numbered frets.

Later, you will find that different keys require adjustments of the tuning known as 'tempering'. This can be done by a combination of moving frets and 'bending' notes as you play, as explained in Appendix 1.

## 2.2. Making a Beautiful Sound

Together with musical phrasing, making a good sound is the most important aspect of viol playing. As Mace (1676) said, 'If you have an unhandsome, rugged, scratching, scraping stroak (as too many have) your viol will seem bad and your play worse.' There is little value in technical facility if the sound you make is not pleasing. Sometimes players concentrate so hard on the notes that they are unaware of making an unpleasant noise. More often, they are dissatisfied with the sound but do not know how to correct or improve it. Or they may have achieved a consistently good sound at moderate speed and medium volume, only to find it deteriorating as soon as they try to play fast passages or widen the dynamic range.

### Tone quality

Three interrelated factors determine the type of sound you produce:
1. Speed of the bow movement

2. Distance of the bow from the bridge
3. Amount of pressure on the string

In general, slow-moving bows need to be nearer the bridge with more pressure, while faster-moving bows should be further from the bridge with less. Playing nearer the bridge gives a more nasal, edgy sound; playing nearer the fingerboard gives a more airy, transparent sound, one that is better suited to softer passages.

If any one factor is fixed by the nature of the music, the others must be adjusted accordingly. Thus a very long note will need a slow bow, which must therefore be quite near the bridge with more than average pressure. Conversely, since the viol speaks more slowly near the bridge, fast notes need to be played slightly further from the bridge, even in loud passages.

These three variables—speed of bow, distance of bow from bridge, and pressure—offer an infinite number of possibilities that give unlimited scope for experimentation. To choose one type of sound for each piece or even each phrase would be to ignore the potential for flexibility and variety in the instrument. Try to make the music more expressive by varying the sounds within each phrase.

## Scratches, scrapes, and squeaks

There are many different reasons for bad sound. Some can be remedied by small adjustments; others require more drastic measures, such as changing strings, or moving the soundpost. Use the following checklist to find the cause of your problem:

1. Not enough contact between hair and string at some point in the stroke.
2. No arm weight in bow: i.e. arm and shoulder not relaxed.
3. Bow too close or too far from bridge.
4. Bow not parallel to bridge.
5. Bow moving too fast or too slowly.
6. Too much pressure, stifling the sound.
7. Left-hand fingers too far behind fret, or over the top of it.
8. Left-hand fingers not pressing hard enough, especially when barring.
9. Too little rosin on bow.
10. Worn-out string, no longer resonating.
11. A 'wolf note': one on a particular string which refuses to speak (see Section 5.2).
12. A poorly made or badly set-up instrument.

*Wrist movement*

There is often confusion about the different types of movement that the wrist has to make. Pushing the wrist in and out (towards and away from the viol) moves the bow forwards and backwards; this movement is in the horizontal plane. Rotating the wrist increases or decreases tension on the hair which alters the tone; this movement should be independent of the first. The two combine in a way that causes the forward stroke (wrist in) to have a tendency towards greater rotation (anticlockwise), resulting in a stronger sound. When the wrist is pulled out, the tendency is to release tension (like a spring) and allow the palm of the hand to face upwards more than on the forward stroke. This gives a weaker backstroke.

You should develop this natural strong–weak bowing, but you also need to be able to play on the forward bow with less tension and the back bow with more.

There is a third movement of the wrist that allows the hand to drop down towards the floor. This is used for fast string crossings, as explained later.

*Bow speed*

Bow speed need not be constant throughout a note—many nuances can be made by increasing or decreasing the speed within a note. Bear in mind that similar laws of friction apply to bowing and driving a car: if you start too fast, the bow will skid, whereas a gentle acceleration will produce a good sound. If more weight is applied before starting to move, the initial bow speed can be faster. Likewise, changing the bow is like driving round a hairpin bend—the better contact you have with the string, the more easily you can turn round without skating. A car moving too slowly in snow will get stuck, whereas one driving too fast will skid.

In general the lower strings need a slower bow speed to start a note as they speak more slowly than the higher ones.

## 2.3. More about Bowing

*Fast notes*

Fast notes are normally played not with the arm but with the wrist or fingers. The quicker the note, the less bow you need. Very quick notes should be played with the fingers alone, as even the wrist is too clumsy to use at speed. In contrast to the technique for longer notes, the hand and fingers now become active and the wrist passive.

Start by resting the bow on one of the middle strings, fairly near the tip, making sure that the middle finger (on the hair) is well bent. Keeping firm pressure on the bow, extend your fingers a little towards the viol, using the muscles in the back of the hand and the bottom joint of the fingers, but not straightening the tip of the middle finger too much. This should cause the bow to move 2–3 cm towards the viol (Fig. 14). Next, pull the fingers back again into a more bent position, so that you end where you started. Note that the middle finger does not slide along the hair, but keeps a firm contact, pushing the bow a small distance in either direction. The angle of the wrist will change, but only as a passive result of the finger movement.

Gradually speed up this movement of the fingers, keeping a constant pressure on the hair and making sure that you give slightly more emphasis to the push movement than to the pull. Practise accenting groups of four or eight notes as shown in Ex. 13. To begin with, hold your wrist and arm steady with your other hand, to make sure that the hand and fingers are doing all the active work, with the wrist and arm passive. The thumb should start in a straight line with the forearm, so that there is no sharp angle at the wrist; this gives greater flexibility in the movement of the fingers. Never let the tip of the middle finger straighten too

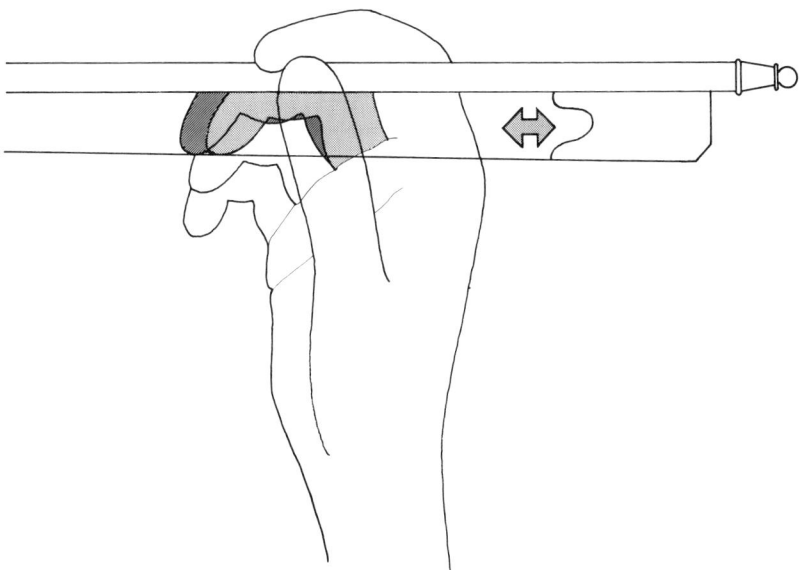

Fig. 14. Movement of the fingers in fast passages

## 2.3. More about Bowing

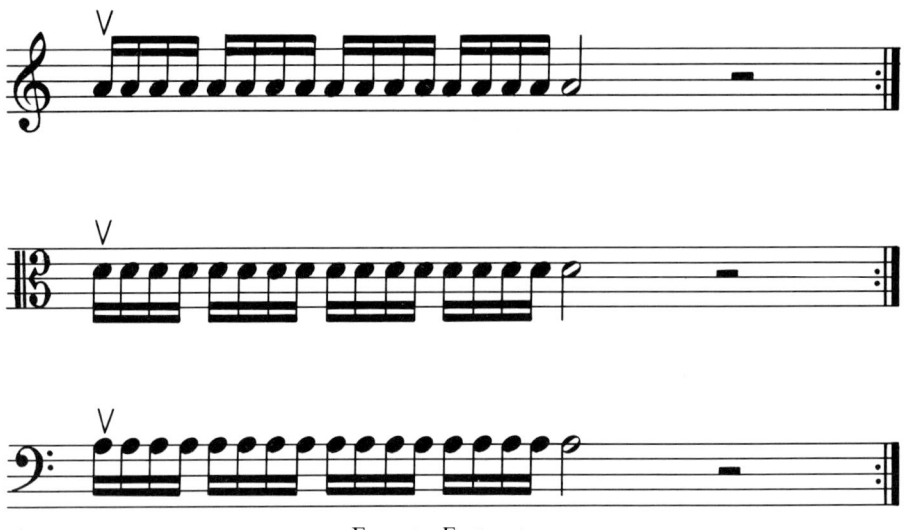

Ex. 13. Fast notes

far, otherwise you will lose control. Try not to increase tension on the hair during the finger movements, as this will cause a little bulge on each note. The movement should be entirely lateral.

Once you have mastered this movement on one note, the next stage is to combine bow and left-hand finger movements. Play groups of four notes on one string (Ex. 14), using the strongest fingers first (Ex. 14a) and progressing to weaker fingers later (Ex. 14b).

Begin by pausing between each note, making sure that bow and left hand move together, but using only a small movement of the bow. Keep the pressure on the hair constant; you will find that this produces a grating sound at the end of each note, but do not be tempted to reduce the pressure—this effect disappears as you play faster. Now gradually speed up until bow and fingers fall out of phase. This usually means that you are failing to lift your fingers off fast enough in descending notes.

When you can co-ordinate well on one string, introduce a string crossing, again using the strongest fingers first. In scale passages like those in Ex. 15 leave the last finger down on the lower string when crossing up, but take off the first finger so that it is ready to go down when it is needed on the upper string; similarly, on the way down put the first finger in place on the lower string before it is actually needed. These silent movements of the first finger are indicated in Ex. 15 by plus and minus signs under the staff. Keep the bow close to both strings and avoid any sudden jerk across the string (see below and Section 1.4).

Ex. 14. Co-ordination on one string

## Dotted notes

As described in Part 1, dotted notes can often be played using a combination of travelling up the bow and light back bows. However, any arm movement on a short back bow is bound to give an unwanted accent, even if very little bow is used. Using the fingers only for the back bow or the short note (usually the same thing) gives a much better feeling of progression through the dotted note.

Try Ex. 16a on any note. Play the dotted note with the arm on the forward

2.3. More about Bowing

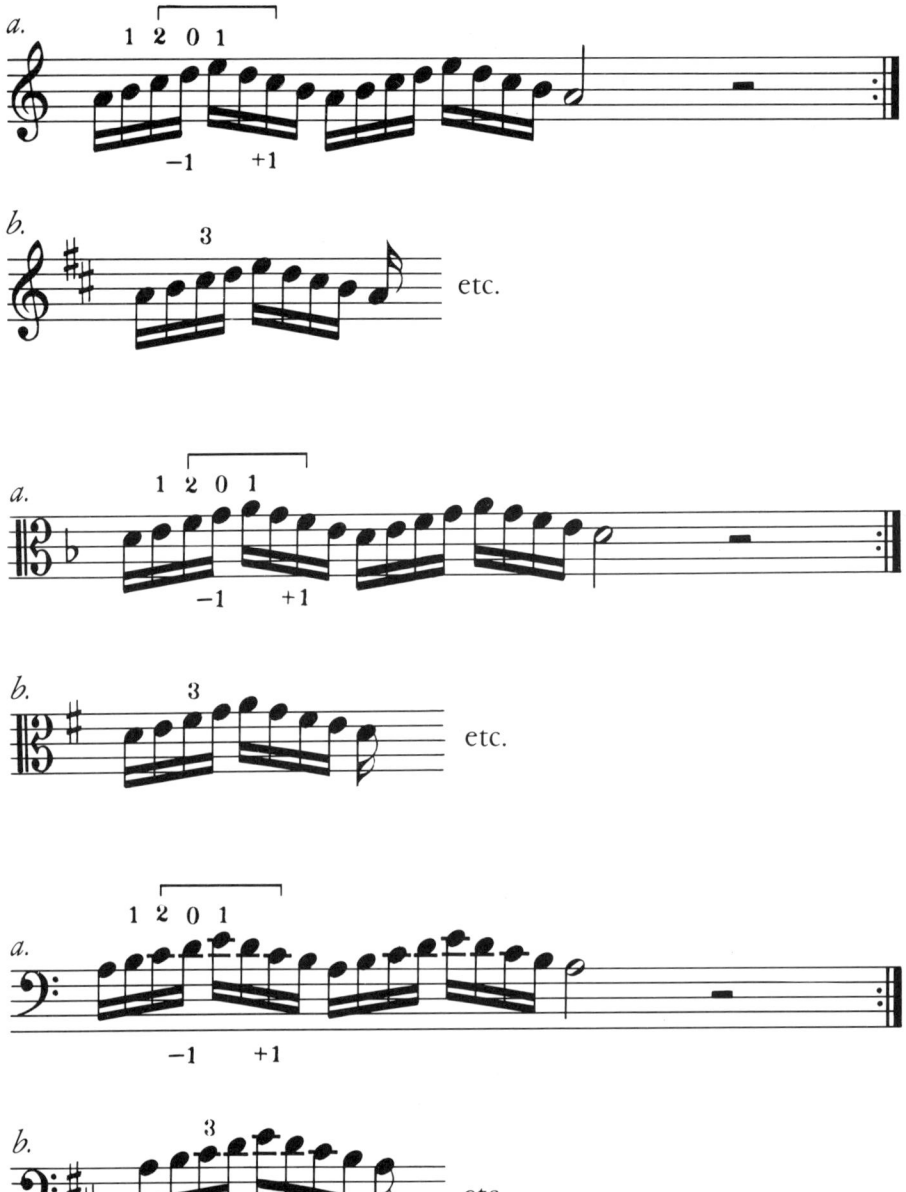

Ex. 15. Co-ordination in string crossing

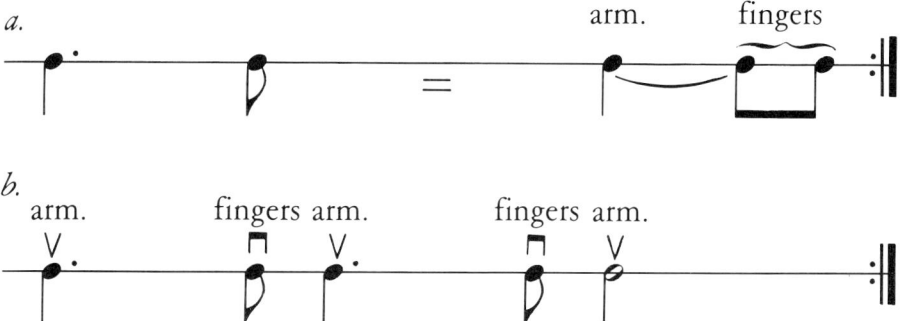

Ex. 16. Finger and arm movement in dotted notes

bow but at the end of the stroke open out the fingers towards the viol, as in the method explained for fast notes. If the forward stroke ends with a fairly open hand, it is then possible to use the fingers alone to pull back, which gives a very light back stroke for the short note. This can be followed by a further arm movement on the following note (Ex. 16b) and the whole phrase will then have a good feeling of line. Try to imagine the arm making a continuous forward movement while the fingers slightly interrupt the sound by pulling briefly in the opposite direction. (This is only possible in passages where there is a suitable place to recover the bow.)

In fast dotted passages both long and short notes can be played with the fingers alone, using the same type of movement as for even fast notes (Ex. 17a). Be especially careful not to tension the hair with the middle finger on the back stroke, as the short note must still be light compared with the long one. In slow dotted passages the arm is needed for both strokes, but the back stroke must still be lighter. It may be a help to move away from the bridge on such occasions (Ex. 17b).

Sometimes it is not possible to arrive at a dotted note on a forward bow. In this case, tuck the next (short) note backwards too, bringing the bowing back to

Ex. 17. Fast and slow dotted notes

## 2.3. More about Bowing

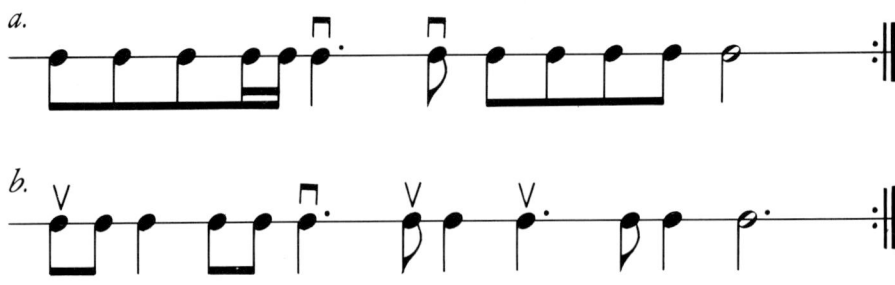

Ex. 18. When to tuck on dotted notes

normal on the following note (Ex. 18a). However, in a passage like the one shown in Ex. 18b this would cause the second dotted note also to be bowed backwards, so it is then best to bow alternately without tucks.

A dotted note followed by a pair of quick notes is better played on a back bow so that the quick notes can be played near the tip of the bow (Ex. 19a). See also Piece 41 in *First Solos*. The same should be done in the case of any long note followed by an even number of faster notes, so that the run can begin on the forward stroke (Ex. 19b).

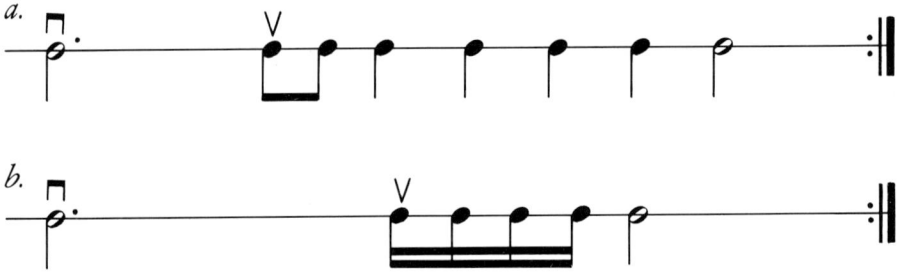

Ex. 19. Bow direction on dotted notes

Practise all the patterns shown in Exx. 16–19, first on one note, then making up phrases to fit the rhythms. Look out for similar patterns in all the pieces you have played. You will find them frequently in consort music, as described in Section 3.2.

### Triplet bowing

Music written in triple time or with internal triple subdivisions (6/8, 6/4, 12/8, triplets) causes bowing problems for which you need to be prepared.

The difficulty with any bowing in groups of three is that the stress has to come alternately on the forward and back bow unless tucks are used. Too much tucking can sound stilted, particularly in fast passages, and it is therefore important to be able to stress equally whichever way you are bowing. In a 6/8 rhythm the forward bows on the third and fifth quavers will make a group of six notes sound as if they are in 3/4 time if those beats are incorrectly stressed.

Practise groups of six notes with alternate bows, making very strong stresses in the two different rhythms shown in Ex. 20.

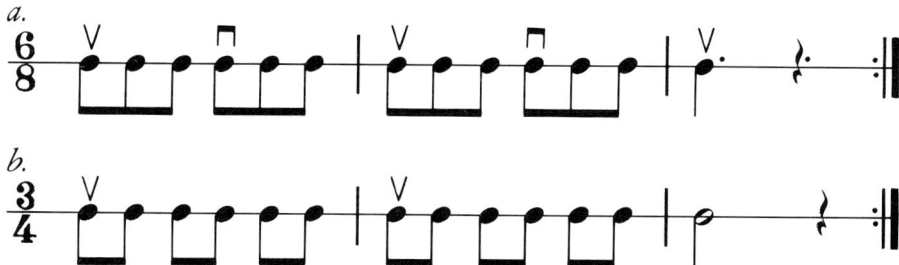

Ex. 20. Triplet bowing

Most dotted notes are best played with a forward bow, as already explained, but, when they form part of a group of three notes, this becomes impossible, since none of the alternatives for tucking works at all well. As a result, this type of grouping also has to be bowed out, as shown in Ex. 21. Make sure that, either way, the short note is played with the fingers only and that the basic arm movement for the whole group is alternately forward and back. Try to stress the dotted note equally, whichever way it comes. See Piece 45 in *First Solos*.

Ex. 21. Dotted notes in triple time

Scales in triplets provide practice in playing groups of three notes with alternating bowing, with the first note of each triplet stressed. Practise this pattern in several different keys, using Ex. 22 as a model.

## Slurring and legato tucking

Slurring is the joining of two or more notes together in one bow stroke. It is often used in Baroque music, more rarely in consort and earlier solo music. To slur any

## 2.3. More about Bowing

Ex. 22. Scales in triplets

notes together, simply keep the bow moving at a constant speed and change fingers as required. Do not be tempted to increase the bow speed where fast notes are slurred together and the left-hand fingers are moving more quickly.

Practise Ex. 23, slurring any pair or larger group of notes, starting as always with the strongest fingers (1 and 2) but not ignoring the weaker combinations (such as 3 and 4). Work out a bow speed and keep it constant, however many notes the fingers have to play; use a metronome to check your accuracy from time to time.

Ex. 23. Slurring

## 2.3. More about Bowing

In slurring, the fingers of the left hand must work very firmly and precisely. They should lift off and be replaced as fast as possible, otherwise you will produce unwanted sounds between the notes. When slurring to an open string, you may need to pluck the string very slightly as you lift the finger off, to make it sound immediately.

You should sometimes practise fingering without the bow; the notes should be quite clearly audible.

Practise the harder patterns in Ex. 24 in groups of four and eight, with the bow starting both forward and back. Before you try each one, play the bowing rhythm on one note, for example ♩ ♩ ♩. Make up further patterns on other strings and in other keys.

Ex. 24. More difficult slurs

It is hard to slur across strings without making an accent or a squeak, so where possible avoid crossing by using a different fingering. For example, use an extension in first position rather than half position, as in Ex. 25.

Note that, whenever you cross strings, whether you are slurring or not, the last finger to be used on the lower string *must* be held down until the next note has begun. Ex. 25d could also be fingered with the fourth finger, but in this case the first must be held while the fourth goes down. Practise these patterns backwards too; the same fingering applies.

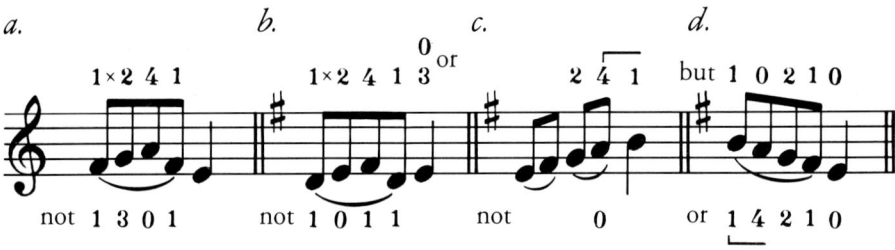

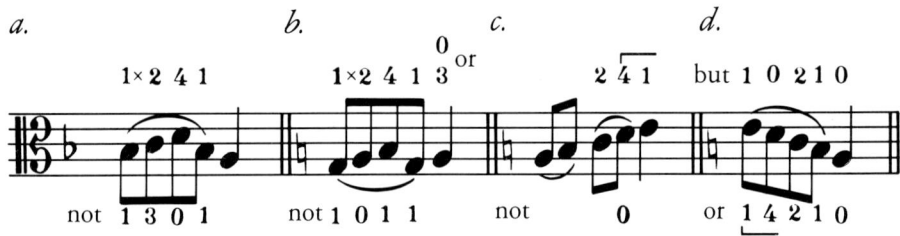

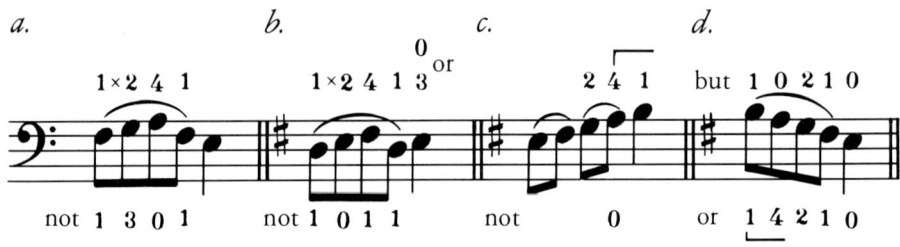

Ex. 25. Slurred string crossing

Where crossing strings during a slur is unavoidable, imagine that on each successive note the bow is getting closer to the next string, so that when the crossover actually happens the movement is minimal. See Sections 3.6 and 3.7 for more difficult examples of slurring across strings.

In running passages which include tucks, the tucked notes can be almost slurred, with only the slightest lightening of pressure between notes. It should be possible to make the tucked notes sound almost indistinguishable from those which are bowed out.

In Ex. 26 the second bowing gives a more noticeable break after the crotchet. Which bowing you choose (*a* or *b*) should depend on the phrasing required. Pieces 49, 50, and 51 in *First Solos* include slurs and fast notes.

There are a few examples in the viol repertoire of slurring on repeated notes. This probably implied a single, pulsating note rather than a succession of

## 2.3. More about Bowing 59

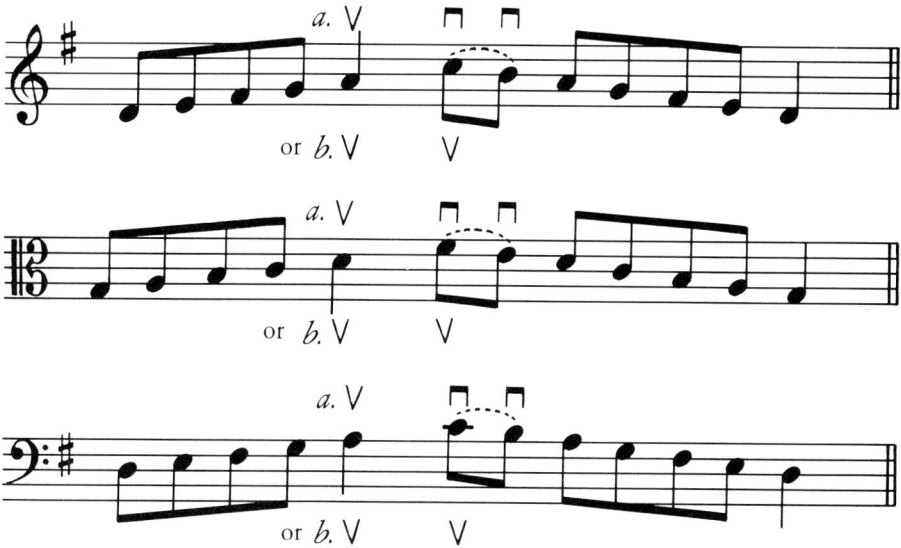

Ex. 26. Tucking on fast notes

separate, repeated notes. Practise the full range of articulation from almost inaudible pulsations of one long note to short repeated notes in one bow.

Ex. 27, based on Jenkins's six-part Pavan, No. 2, demonstrates the use of tucking as a musical effect rather than a way of correcting the bowing. The passage occurs in the second section of the piece and is divided between the top four parts. It is not very fast, and should sound like pulsating crotchets rather than separate quavers. Practise Ex. 27, being careful not to stop the bow while tucking. See Ex. 69 for an example of this type of bowing at a faster speed.

Ex. 27. Legato tucking

## 2.3. More about Bowing

### String crossing and resonance

The basic technique of string crossing was described in Section 1.4. The next stage is to maintain resonance between the notes. Think of the bow stroke as a curve up or down and not as two separate movements along and up (Fig. 15). This should enable you to end the bow stroke on the next string up or down, and, if the stroke is done correctly, the string you have just played will still be

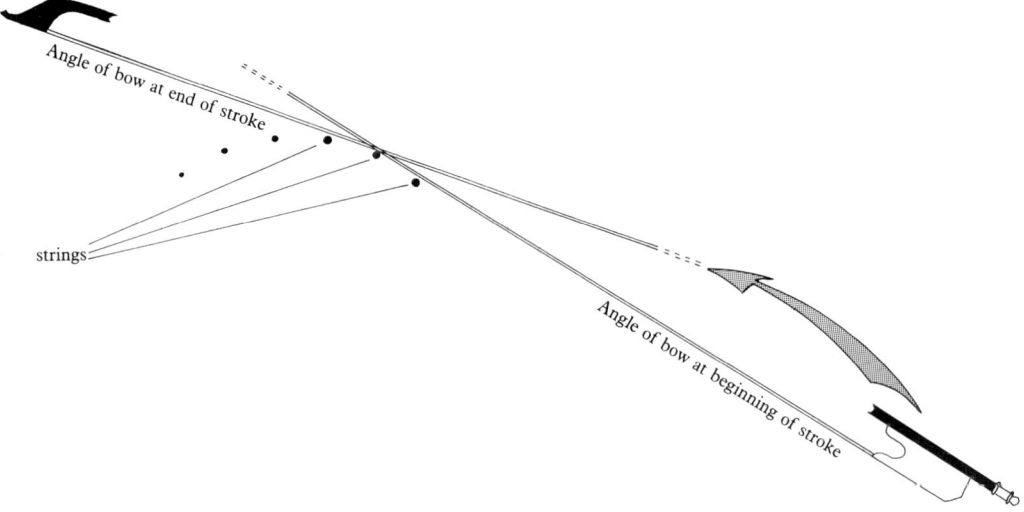

Fig. 15. The bow stroke when string crossing

resonating. Make sure you do not stop the bow on the first string before crossing, otherwise it will go dead. Play the bottom string and move over to rest on the fifth so that the first note continues to ring. If it does not, play the same note again and lift the bow off. This should show how much resonance is possible, and you should aim to get just as much when you cross to another string (Ex. 28).

Use fairly short bows and try to come to rest gently on the upper string without sounding the note. Continue upwards in the same way to the top string,

2.3. More about Bowing   61

Ex. 28. Resonance

pausing each time to listen for the resonance. You should be able to play all six notes forward without any retaking. Come down in the same way on back bows. It is much harder bowing the opposite way, but it should still be possible to play six notes in one bow. The tendency is to use far too much bow when crossing strings. The first priority in this exercise is to get every note to ring; the second is to avoid crashing into the next string.

## *Jumping strings*

To jump one or more strings, do not lift the bow off into the air but use the intervening strings as a fulcrum on which to rock the bow, maintaining some pressure all the time. You may be reluctant to do this at first for fear of sounding unwanted strings, but, provided the bow does not actually move forwards or backwards while touching the intervening strings, they will not sound. Experiment with this.

Begin by stopping on the adjacent string, allowing the first to ring before crossing to the next string to be played. Practise playing any pair of open strings, including first and sixth, and always pause long enough between notes to see if they are resonating properly. Turn back to Section 1.4, simple string crossing, to check that your arm movement is correct.

Practising octave leaps is a useful exercise for string crossing as these appear very frequently in all viol music. They are particularly common in continuo parts (see Section 3.3). In Ex. 29 hold each finger down until you have to move it. In the slowest part of the exercise, cross to the fifth string at the end of the first note, allowing it to ring into the rest. During the rest, rock the bow up to the fourth string to prepare for the next note by gripping the string. Do the opposite going down, and gradually speed up until you can play quavers and still make a good beginning on each note. Ex. 29 is based on an extract from Marin Marais's *Sonnerie de Ste Geneviève*. When you can play it with confidence, attempt the original Marais (Ex. 30), in which the same passage appears in fast semiquavers.

Note that, whatever the duration of the notes, the crossing movement should be fast. So, for example, crossing between minims should be as fast as crossing between semiquavers, though obviously for fast notes the duration of each note is shorter and the gaps between notes are correspondingly smaller.

## *Fast string crossings*

In fast playing the normal arm movements used in string crossing can become very cumbersome. It is possible to reduce the amount of movement needed by an

2.3. More about Bowing 63

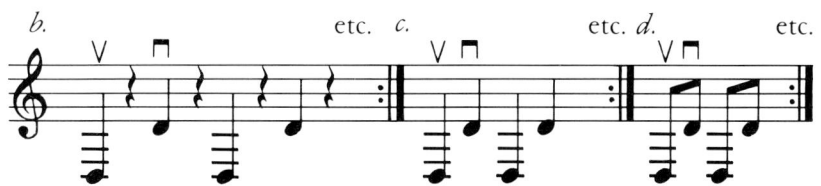

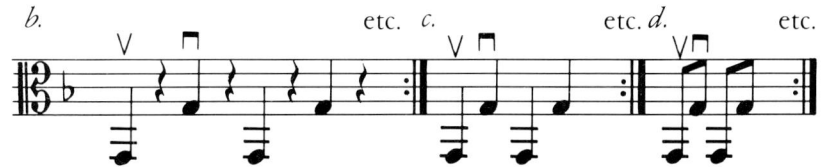

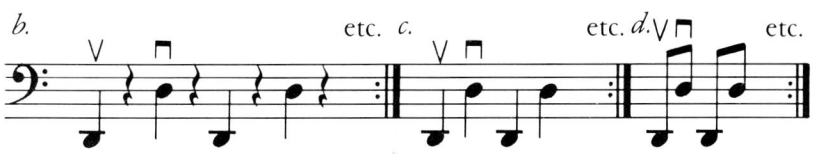

Ex. 29. Octaves

64   2.3. *More about Bowing*

Ex. 30. Octaves in semiquavers

up-and-down motion of the hand that tilts the bow more or less on to the edge of the hair.

Start with the bow very much tipped away on the lower of the two strings to be crossed, so that the stick is almost resting on the string (Fig. 16a). Keep the bow as close as possible to the next string up. Now lift the hand so that it is almost level with the wrist and forearm (Fig. 16b). You should find that the bow has moved up to the next string, and that the hair of the bow is much flatter on the string.

Practise this up-and-down movement of the hand without moving the bow along the string. Watch the bow where it rests on the string: you should see the pressure changing from the lower to the upper string. When you are satisfied with the movement, begin to move the bow forwards and backwards as usual.

Begin with a forward bow on the lower string, and as you play, lift your hand so that you end the stroke with the bow resting on the upper string (Ex. 31). In the same way, as you make the back stroke, drop the hand so that you end on the lower string. You may need to move the arm very slightly to help the crossing. Gradually speed up all these actions until the hand is moving in a continuous circle, as if whipping cream.

For further practice in string crossing, extend Ex. 31 to include slurring across two strings, and subsequently both slurring and bowing out across three and four strings. (See also Exx. 44, 64, and 67.)

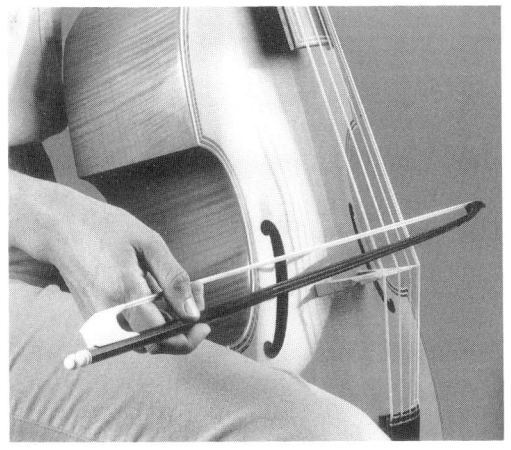

*a.* lower string            *b.* upper string

Fig. 16. Hand and bow position for fast string crossing.

Ex. 31. String crossings using the hand

## 2.4. More Difficult Fingerings

*Shifting*

Shifting means changing the left-hand position on the fingerboard to a higher or lower fret. Most consort playing requires frequent movement between half and first position combined with extensions, and only the occasional shift on the top string up to the highest fret or beyond is needed. Solo music tends to use a much wider range and therefore involves many more shifts into high positions, up to one and a half octaves above the open string.

One of the main aims in viol technique is to avoid jumping fingers, which causes gaps in the sound and loss of resonance. If you are moving between first and half positions, it is sometimes possible to shift the hand while playing an open string. Otherwise the shift can be made by a combination of extensions and contractions using a caterpillar-like motion of the fingers to crawl into the new position (see Section 1.4). This may be more difficult in higher positions, but the same principles should be applied where possible.

With smaller instruments, such as the treble and to a lesser extent the tenor, you can use extensions between all fingers to avoid jumping up to the top fret. There are strongly opposed views on whether this is desirable, and on treble fingering in general. Should the treble viol be played chromatically like the bass, that is with one finger to a fret and occasional extensions, or diatonically, with one finger to each note of the scale, using extensions wherever necessary? Diatonic fingering can be used to minimize shifting and string crossing, and the finger spacing is similar to that required for playing the bass (Fig. 17). However, many people find the necessary hand position awkward and prefer to play all sizes of viol in the same way, using basically chromatic fingering but with occasional extensions where this avoids a difficult shift. You should choose whatever fingering feels most comfortable.

In Ex. 32 jumping can be avoided by using the crawling motion described above, and illustrated in Fig. 18. When crawling, or shifting while playing an open string, you should move the thumb with the rest of the hand so that it remains opposite the second finger rather than being left behind. In some cases it may be easier to move the thumb a little earlier or later than the other fingers.

*How and where to shift*

There are occasions when jumping the hand is unavoidable. In that case the whole hand should move as a unit. As mentioned above, the thumb should always remain opposite the second finger.

2.4. More Difficult Fingerings   67

Fig. 17. Diatonic fingering on the treble viol

Fig. 18. Contracted fingering

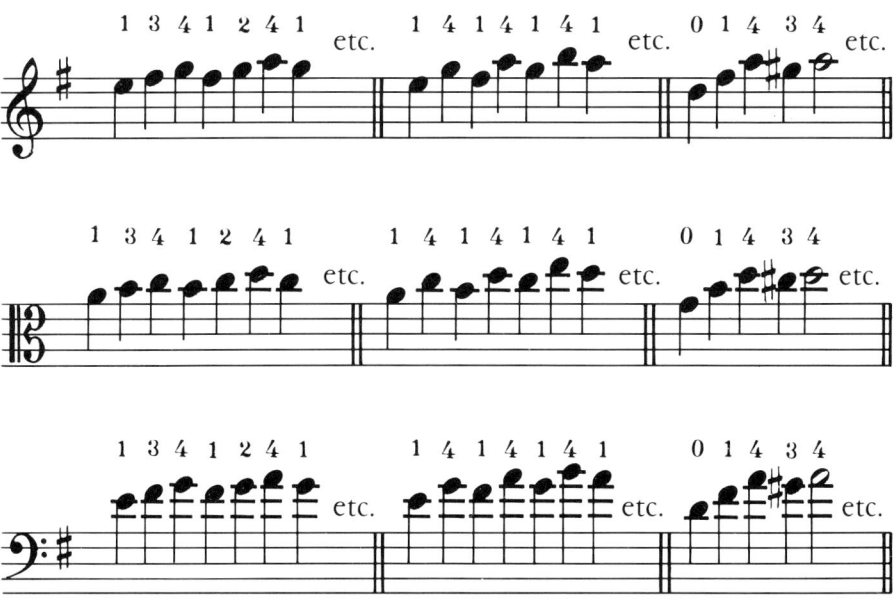

Ex. 32. Crawling

## 2.4. More Difficult Fingerings

Although frets make it easier to find the new position accurately, they also make it more difficult to move smoothly. You will find that during the shift it is necessary to lighten finger and thumb pressure on the neck.

When shifting up to a higher note, let the whole arm fall with gravity, keeping the left-hand position at right angles to the neck. In shifting down to a lower note, pull the wrist back a little towards the pegs to prepare the movement of the hand.

Make sure that the bow is stationary while the actual shifting movement takes place, otherwise there will be extraneous sounds of departure and arrival. When the shift involves a string crossing, move the bow to the new string before moving any fingers.

In certain keys the shift on the top string to the top fret requires a simultaneous backward extension, as for example when the third fret is needed as opposed to the fourth. In this case the whole hand (including the thumb) moves up two frets, while the first finger drags behind and moves up only one.

When a shift to another position is necessary, there are often several possible places where it can be made. It is important to decide where to move for musical reasons rather than at random. The following points should be considered:

1. Shift between phrases whenever possible, as the gap can then be a positive factor and actually assist the phrasing.
2. Shifting after a long note gives you more time to move; for example, it will usually be better to move after a dotted note than after the short note following it.
3. Any shift gives a little accent, so try to move on to strong beats, that is, notes which need stress (not necessarily the first beat in the bar).
4. Shifting between semitones involves smaller movements and can therefore be done unobtrusively.

Ex. 33 shows three passages which run up to the top fret in even notes. Clearly, the possibility of shifting after a long note is precluded, so the choice is between moving on a semitone or on to a strong beat. On the treble viol, the use of diatonic fingering would avoid any shift at all.

Ex. 33a shows the ideal situation where shifting on a semitone coincides with arrival on a strong beat. The only complication arises from the fact that the top three notes are in extended position, so that the shift is really of a whole tone rather than a semitone, with the first finger dragging behind as described earlier. Make sure that the thumb moves to the fifth fret to keep the correct hand position.

Ex. 33b is more problematic, since shifting on the semitone could cause an

## 2.4. More Difficult Fingerings 69

Ex. 33. Alternative routes to the top fret

unwanted stress on a very weak beat. It might be better to shift one note later, again on to the strong beat.

Ex. 33c shows two possibilities for shifting on to the strong beat, the first one probably being the best. It also illustrates a third way of shifting up, using the open string and then crossing down a string while moving into the higher position. This is more complicated for the bow but gives the fingers more time to move and is sometimes easier in very fast runs.

All these fingerings should also be practised in reverse for downward shifts which, surprisingly, are often harder to manage. The thumb must always move as well, but, as already suggested, it need not move at exactly the same time as the fingers. See Exx. 57, 58, and 60 for further illustrations of where to shift.

The same principles apply when you shift into even higher positions. When more than one shift is required in a single phrase, try to play at least two notes in one position, except where this would conflict with the musical considerations explained above. See Section 3.4 for more advice on playing in high positions.

## Double stopping

The viol, like all fretted instruments, is particularly well suited to playing double stops (two notes sounded together) and chords. Both occur at least occasionally in the majority of works in the solo repertoire.

The most common intervals to be found in passages that include double stopping are thirds and sixths. Although it might seem simplest always to use the strongest fingers, this would make it necessary to jump and thus cause noticeable gaps in the sound. Ex. 34 shows how to eliminate jumps by using all fingers.

Practise each pair of thirds over and over again until your fingers fall easily into place. Then practise them slurred so that you can hear if the pairs of fingers are moving together. Increase speed gradually until co-ordination fails, then play more slowly again. In time you should be able to play whole scales in double-stopped thirds.

Do not be tempted to press any harder than usual just because you are bowing two notes at once. There is a tendency to do this in sympathy with the left hand, which has to exert more pressure when barring or holding down two notes at a time. As a result, double-stopped notes often sound scratchy. The remedy is to bow exactly as you would when playing single notes. It may be helpful to practise just the top or bottom part of pieces that include a lot of double stopping, using the same fingers as you would when playing all the notes (see Ex. 63).

If you have to play consecutive double stops, try to make use of all four fingers, as explained above; this minimizes the need to jump from one chord to the next.

## 2.4. More Difficult Fingerings

Ex. 34. Double stopping in thirds

Where jumping is unavoidable, allow the sound to die a little between notes so that the jumps do not sound so obvious. Try not to slide from one chord to the next.

### Larger chords

The same basic principles apply to chords of more than two notes. It is first essential to find a fingering that uses a different string for each note, so that the fingers can be held down for the duration of the chord. This may sometimes mean finding a substitute for an open string.

Ex. 35 gives fingerings for some of the chords most frequently found in viol music. You may have to turn your wrist back to get all the fingers in line, but do not lift the elbow or arm more than necessary (Fig. 19).

For large chords, such as D major across six strings, you will need three fingers on the same fret. It may be impossible to get all the fingers absolutely in line and right up to the fret, but make sure that the finger on the highest string is not allowed to go over the top of the fret. It is better to have the lowest finger slightly further back to make room for the other two. Practise strumming the chords with the thumb to see if they resonate properly. This will show up any bad placement of fingers.

## 2.4. More Difficult Fingerings

Ex. 35. Common chords

Fig. 19. Fingering for the D major chord

When bowing chords, begin by sounding the bass note alone, then cross upwards using very little bow and allowing the pressure to lighten as you move, so that you end on the top note hardly any further up the bow than where you started. The distance between the strings is enough to sound each note.

Large chords are best played with a forward bow, since the forward movement is in the same direction as the crossing movement and the bow length is regained as you move. In sequences of chords, try to get the most prominent (usually the largest) on the forward bow and allow the others to follow alternately.

In chords with the interval of a fourth at the top, hold the highest note only, since sounding the top two notes together after the rest of the chord has died away will produce the effect of second inversion (unless another instrument is providing the bass). If the top two notes make intervals of a second, third, fifth, or sixth, however, keep both notes sounding.

Occasionally, three-note chords need to be played with all three notes together. To do this, play further away from the bridge where there is less tension on the strings. You will need to use a fast bow to compensate for the extra pressure required.

For most chords, the speed of spread depends on the duration of the chord and the tempo. Short chords should in general be spread more quickly than longer ones, but not where this would disrupt the peaceful character of a slow movement. Do not be afraid to linger on the bass note. This is often appropriate musically and also allows you more time to put down fingers for the upper notes, rather than leaving a gap before the chord while you try to find all the notes at once.

Pausing before chords is a very common fault which interrupts the rhythmic flow and obscures the melodic line. To overcome this problem, practise each chord in a sequence together with the note or chord that precedes it, going backwards and forwards without a break. Play as shown in Ex. 36, based on an extract from Marais, *Cloches ou carillons*.

The exercise breaks down the chord sequence into ten stages. Note that at *d* the whole hand moves up two frets without changing shape. Having mastered one pair of chords, move on to the next so that the second chord becomes the first of the new pair. Eventually, the fingers will fall into place without conscious thought on your part, and you will be able to play the passage without reducing speed or hesitating before the hardest chords. Exx. 48, 56, 64, and 65 provide more practice in playing chords and chord progressions.

74  2.4. More Difficult Fingerings

Ex. 36. Practising chords

2.4. More Difficult Fingerings 75

Ex. 36. (cont.)

## 2.5. Notation

*Playing in different clefs*

Up to this point, all the exercises in the book have been given in the three clefs most commonly used for the three main sizes of viol: treble clef for treble viol, alto clef for tenor viol, and bass clef for bass viol.

Once past the elementary stage, however, you will find that it is not enough to be conversant only with the single clef associated with your size of instrument. Certainly in solo music, and to a lesser extent in consort music, you will need to play in several different clefs. At informal playing sessions, especially if they include wind and plucked instruments as well as viols, you are quite likely to be asked to play bass or tenor viol from the treble clef. Lower tenor parts in consort music are often taken by bass viols but are always written in the alto clef, and works that were played on the cello before the current revival of interest in authentic instruments are sometimes published in tenor clef.

In order not to restrict your playing options, you should try as soon as possible to learn to read fluently all the most frequently used clefs. The following are regularly found in viol music (those in brackets are less common).

Treble viol:   treble (alto)
Tenor viol:    alto, treble, octave treble—treble transposed down an octave (bass)
Bass viol:     bass, alto, octave treble (tenor)

If you want to play from facsimile you will need to become familiar with a number of clefs in addition to those already listed. There are two further C clefs, soprano and mezzo-soprano; the French violin clef; and the baritone clef. The one you are most likely to encounter is the soprano clef, which is used by Christopher Simpson in his 'Divisions for the Practice of Learners'.

The three G clefs, four C clefs, and two F clefs are shown in Fig. 20.

Learning to read an unfamiliar clef often presents unexpected difficulties. Even playing from a familiar clef on a different instrument can be problematic. For example, a cellist well used to the tenor clef will probably find it just as hard as anyone else, at least at first, to play the bass viol from tenor clef rather than the more usual alto. Treble clef on tenor viol can seem completely baffling.

The best strategy in tackling a new clef is to choose a few marker notes that you can easily remember. Then relate these notes to their place on the instrument; e.g. on tenor viol in alto clef, top line = G = top string. From there

G clefs

C clefs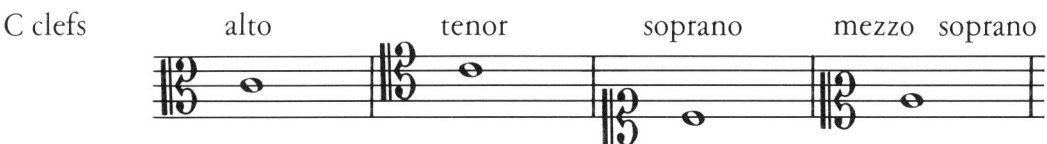

F clefs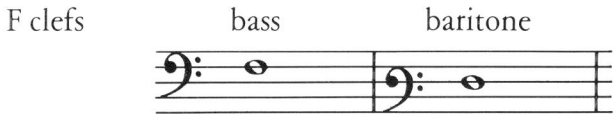

Fig. 20. Clefs used in viol music

play by interval, as in sight-singing, using the marker notes—normally the open strings—to help in the larger leaps. Write in the fingerings until you feel confident about reading the clef. It is a good idea at the beginning to try to play exclusively in the new clef for some time, and certainly to stick to one clef in each playing session.

If you play all sizes of viol, you can sometimes find a trick for reading a difficult clef. For example, playing tenor viol from the mezzo-soprano clef is like playing treble viol in treble clef or bass viol in octave treble clef. Similar tricks can also enable you to transpose if required: for instance if you imagine you are playing a bass while actually playing a tenor, you will be transposing up a fourth. As an interim measure, this sort of tactic is extremely useful, but it is not without risk: it is easy to be caught out by accidentals, since you may be unaware of what notes you are actually playing. In the long term, you should aim to be able to recognize and name the notes in the different clefs. The plainchants in Exx. 37 and 38 can be used to practise reading in different clefs and transposing, as can all the tunes in *First Solos*.

## Reading from fascimile

A large amount of music has recently been made more accessible by the publication of original manuscripts or engravings in fascimile. Although at present most of this is solo music, an increasing amount of music for consort is becoming available. In addition, such material can be obtained from library collections on microfilm. This provides the opportunity to play music as yet unpublished, or, in cases where the music is available in published editions, to compare the edited text with the original.

Apart from the visual appearance of the music, which will seem strange to begin with, reading from facsimile presents no insurmountable problems, though it does need a certain amount of practice. The main differences between viol music as originally notated and as currently transcribed include the following: unfamiliar clefs, the absence of regular barring, the way in which notes are grouped, the types of rest, and coloration—a peculiarity of notation occasionally encountered in triple time.

Most sixteenth- and early seventeenth-century music is either unbarred or has bar lines at unpredictable intervals. On a practical note, this makes it advisable to add rehearsal letters so that you do not continually have to return to the beginning if you have to stop. Equally, the absence of bar lines makes it essential to choose a basic pulse—probably minim or semibreve—for the whole piece. This is especially important for counting rests, but also has a bearing on another feature resulting from the lack of barring—that is the absence of any tied notes. While you will probably find that this helps you to play the frequent cross-rhythms more naturally, it can also make it more difficult to return to the main beat. Despite the initial strangeness, however, there is an enjoyable freedom about playing music without the constraint of bar lines.

The irregular grouping of notes is another source of difficulty. In modern editions, shorter note values are usually grouped according to the prevailing beat. This is rarely the case in early printed music, where quavers and semiquavers are often printed singly or grouped completely at random. In addition, new lines of music will often begin on a weak beat rather than the expected strong one.

Rests can be a problem in reading from facsimile, since they are often rather small and can easily be mistaken for smudges—smudges can also be mistaken for rests! Minim and semibreve rests are the same as in modern notation; a whole space filled represents a rest of a breve (equal to two semibreves); a block spanning two spaces indicates a rest equal to two breves, and so on.

Most consort music was printed in part books rather than in score (see Fig. 21 for an example of a typical consort part). The four basic parts are usually called cantus, altus, tenor, and bassus, with quintus and sextus added in five- and six-part music. The last two parts may be of any range. To choose the size of viol appropriate to a particular musical part, look at the top and bottom notes of that part and use the viol size for which most of the music lies in the best part of the

Fig. 21. Holborne, *Image of Melancholly* (facsimile)

# 2.6. Different Bow Holds

instrument. In sixteenth-century music this could well mean giving the top line to the tenor viol or, in five-part music, using one treble, one tenor, and three basses.

A completely different system of notation you may come across is tablature, where six lines represent the strings and finger positions are indicated by letters or numbers. This was mainly used for lyra-viol music, which is discussed in Section 3.5, and advice on reading tablature is given there.

## 2.6. Different Bow Holds

It is clear from the surviving treatises on the viol that there were many conflicting ideas about technical points such as bowing and fingering, and even more fundamentally, on how to hold the bow.

The bow hold suggested in Section 1.1 basically derives from that advocated by Simpson (1659), but incorporates points from a number of other sources, and is suitable for all types of music. However, you may at this stage find it interesting to try a later development, the so-called 'French' hold. This is described by J.-B. Forqueray (1767), who advises the player to put the middle finger right over the hair, so that the top joint is bent over and the hair lies in the crease (Fig. 22a). This

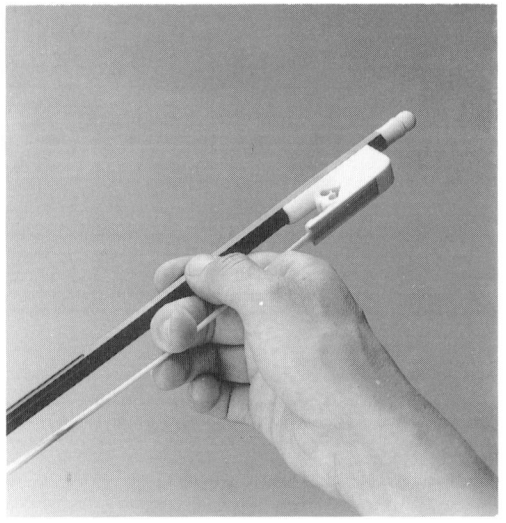
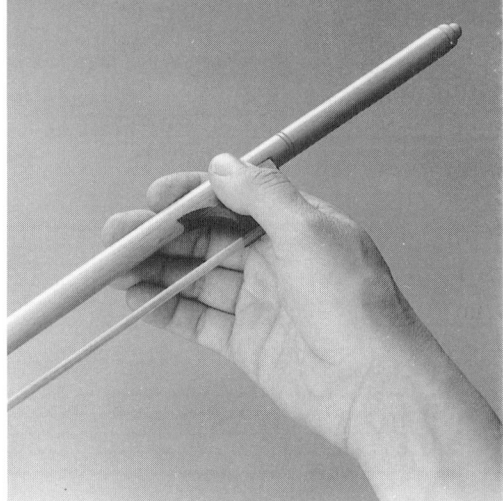

22a. French    22b. Ganassi

Fig. 22. Bow holds

## 2.6. Different Bow Holds

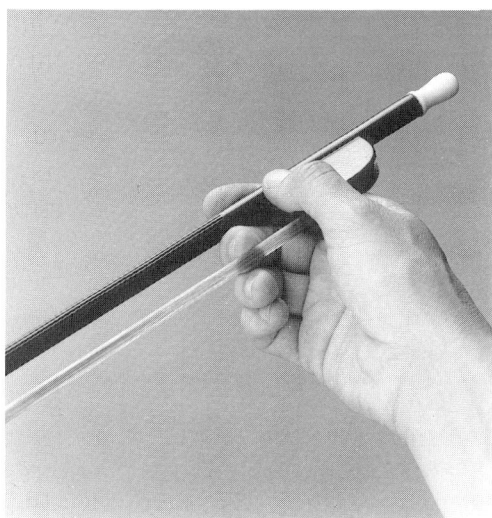

22c. English

Fig. 22 (cont.)

means that it is possible to pull down on the hair much more firmly, which is useful for solo playing. To lift the bow it is then necessary either to support the lower edge of the hair with the ring finger, or to hold the stick more firmly between thumb and index finger, or to use a combination of both.

The various methods of holding the bow were obviously suited to the bows of the period in which they were developed. Renaissance (fixed frog) bows generally have a much deeper frog, which makes it harder to tension the hair in the normal way, and Ganassi (1542–3) clearly describes how the bow should be held without any fingers on the hair but with two fingers on the stick and the thumb on the frog (Fig. 22b) Some of the English writers also recommend holding the bow on the frog, but with one or sometimes two fingers on the hair (Fig. 22c).

As time went on, the bow hold seems to have become increasingly concerned with controlling the hair rather than the stick for varying the sound. According to Forqueray, the bow 'expresses all the emotions, arouses the soul and gives character to all kinds of music', and it is the middle finger on the hair which provides that 'great force of expression which distinguishes all music'.

# 3
# Exploring the Viol Repertoire

## 3.1. Varieties of Music for the Viol

The viol repertoire spans a period of approximately three hundred years, from c.1480 to c.1770. It includes a large amount of solo music, both with and without accompaniment, ensemble music for two to seven viols, chamber music for viol and other instruments, and music for viols and voices in various combinations. Much of this music is now quite easily available, either in modern editions or in facsimile reprints. There is also a small body of modern works, although the viol has attracted considerably less attention from twentieth-century composers than the recorder. Appendix 3 lists a wide selection of available viol music, and you should refer to this while working through Part 3, as well as to the Bibliography and Discography.

 This part of the book is designed to introduce you to all the main types of music for viol. It assumes that you have acquired a basic technique and want to know how to approach the different styles of music, though it is not possible to cover every aspect of viol playing in detail. The examples are not always arranged in order of difficulty, so you can choose where to begin. Less experienced players will probably want to start with the section on consort music. Although nearly all the examples are for bass viol, the technical advice given is relevant to all sizes of instrument, and most of the exercises are easily transposed. There is a comparatively small amount of music written for treble viol solo, but reference is made to this in the appropriate sections wherever it exists. The section on lyra viol should be of particular interest to tenor players, since they have no solo repertoire of their own.

## 3.2. Consort Music

Once you have mastered the basic principles of bowing and fingering, you will be able to start playing viol consorts. Much consort music was written to be played with friends at home and is therefore not too demanding for amateur music-making.

Most ensemble music of the fifteenth and sixteenth centuries does not specify instrumentation, and can certainly be played by a consort of viols or by a mixed ensemble of viols and other instruments. Vocal music of this period can also be performed instrumentally or in combination with voices, depending on the forces available.

By the beginning of the seventeenth century many English composers were writing music specifically for viols. Holborne's collection of dances published in 1599 is for 'Viols, Violins or other Musicall Wind Instruments', but composers writing only slightly later, such as Gibbons, Jenkins, Lupo, and Coprario, definitely intended that their music should be played on viols.

The two main types of English consort music are the dance—which comes in many different forms: pavan, galliard, courante, almain, sarabande, and ayre—and the fantasy. Pavans are probably the easiest pieces to start with since they are usually fairly slow moving and the notes and rhythm are often quite straightforward. Fantasies present greater difficulties, including more passages with fast notes and complex rhythms which makes it harder to keep your place.

However, there are a number of fantasy-like pieces based on a cantus firmus, a tune moving in long, slow notes, which is usually confined to one part. These provide an excellent way of allowing a beginner to join a group of more experienced players without feeling that they are being limited to elementary music. The best known of these tunes are the *In nomine*, a plainsong used by Taverner in his mass 'Gloria tibi Trinitas', and *La Spagna*, used by many composers of the fifteenth and sixteenth centuries. These are given in Exx. 37 and 38. The melodies are to be found in a variety of keys and pitches. They provide useful practice in many different facets of technique, including bow control, clef reading, and transposition. The speed varies from slow to extremely slow. One *In nomine* by Tye is written in 5/4 throughout, each note of the plainsong having the rhythm semibreve–crotchet, a very good bowing exercise.

## Tuning in consort

Even the best playing can be ruined by one out-of-tune string, and it is therefore essential to spend time tuning in order to have an enjoyable consort session.

The most reliable method of tuning a consort is as follows: first the person in the group with the best ear should tune completely, as described in Section 2.1. Preferably this should be done on a bass viol, as it is easier for others to hear the pitch. Then each player should tune in turn, string by string to the bass. This may seem a longwinded procedure compared with the common practice of tuning

84   3.2. Consort Music

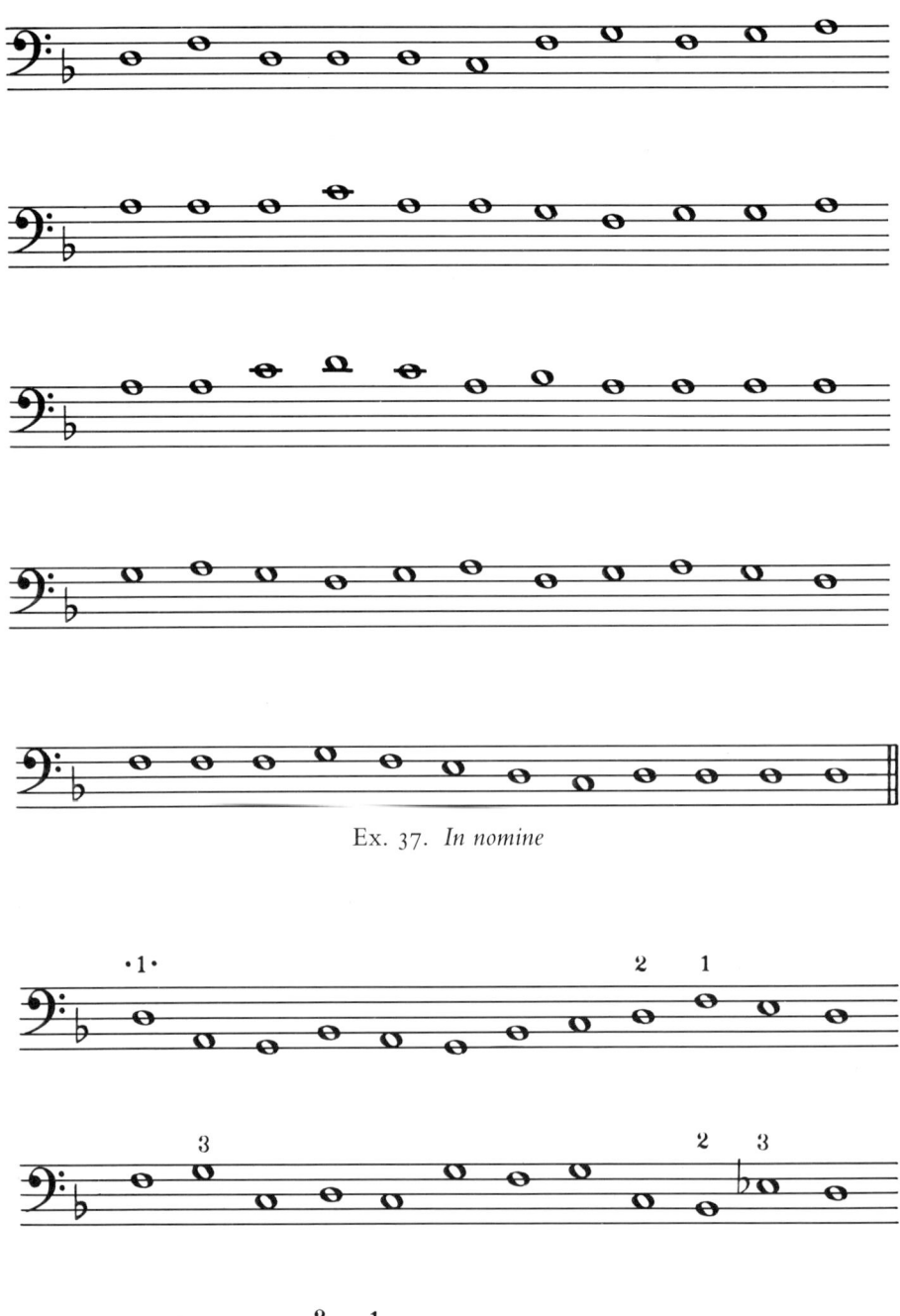

Ex. 37. *In nomine*

Ex. 38. *La Spagna*

individually to an agreed pitch. However, it will be found that each person has a different idea of how intervals should sound, and this can produce discrepancies with the other strings. (The reasons for this are explained in Appendix 1, where more detailed advice on tuning will be found.)

If you are confident about tuning unisons, fifths, and octaves, it is also possible for one player to play up a scale on the A string and each of the other players to tune open strings to that (for example, A to A, E to B, C to C, G to D, and D to D). This method has an advantage if tuning is very unstable since only one string is used to give all the notes.

You will notice that some pieces call for a bottom C on the bass viol; it was common practice in seventeenth-century England to tune the sixth string down a tone from D to C and finger accordingly.

## Dance music

Each dance form has its own distinctive character and needs to be played in an appropriate style, though the same name can imply something quite different according to the period when the piece was written. Some points to note in playing the most common dance forms are given below.

Pavans are usually played at a fairly slow tempo, but do not be tempted to slow down further at the end of every section. Save this for the last repeat of the last section.

The length of the final note of each section should depend to a certain extent on the speed of the music and on the acoustic you are playing in, but in general take a little time out of the last note to allow breath between sections.

Try to work out the bowing so that not every player has to retake the bow between sections, otherwise the gap will be too noticeable. Bowing may have to be varied on the repeats so that the bow is going the right way for the next section.

Look out especially for phrases (perhaps only a few notes) that imitate another part, as shown in Ex. 39, from Holborne's pavan, *The Funerals*. Begin your 'point' at a dynamic that continues logically from the previous player's; the overall effect should be of a continuous musical line. Try to count pavans in the longest possible beats. For example, if the time signature is 4/2, try to feel two semibreves in a bar rather than four minims. This helps avoid too many accents, which can make pavans sound static and lumpy.

The galliard is a more lively dance in triple rhythm. It is sometimes barred in three but should generally be stressed in six, subdivided into two groups of three or sometimes three groups of two. Look to see where the first main stress should

Ex. 39. Holborne, *The Funerals*

be: it will not necessarily be on the first note, and need not always be the same in each part. In general the longer notes should be given greater stress, particularly at changes of harmony. To avoid monotony, do not accent each group of notes equally, but vary the stress according to the musical importance of the phrase. To bring out the cross-rhythms of 6/4 against 3/2, accent the beginnings of the strong notes and play the rest much more lightly. Let the sound die away without stopping the bow too abruptly. A useful rehearsal device is for all players to pluck rather than bow their parts. This allows the complex rhythms to be heard more clearly.

Plucking can also suggest the dance-like character appropriate to this type of music. When the players take up their bows again they should try to recreate the lighter feel of the sound they have just heard. Almost always this results in a much clearer, livelier performance.

In many galliards barred in three the first bar leads to the second, the third to the fourth, and so on, but often bars 4 and 8 are ends of phrases, and the whole section can become a double arch. This shape is more obvious when barred in six, as shown in Fig. 23. As when playing pavans, try to feel long beats rather than short. So in 3/4 or 6/4, think of minims and dotted minims rather than crotchets, but also think more broadly, in semibreve and dotted semibreve beats.

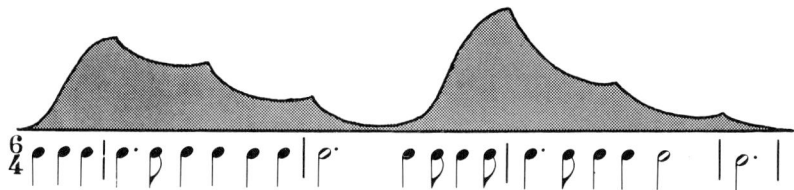

Fig. 23. The shape of the first strain of a galliard

You should vary the repeats in dance forms. This can be done in several ways, for example by contrast of dynamics, different articulation, or by adding decoration. Players of the time would have been expected to elaborate their parts with 'divisions', and you will find that you can do this with practice. Exx. 40 and 41 give sections from a pavan by Tomkins and a galliard by Holborne (*Muy*

Ex. 40. Tomkins, Pavan à 5

Ex. 41. Holborne, *Muy Linda*

*Linda*), first as notated and then with divisions. Play these, and then try to make up some variations of your own. The simplest types of division are those created by filling in the gaps between notes a third apart, resulting in stepwise motion and the subdivision of the written note into two notes of half the value (see Ex. 41, bar 1). Where the motion is already stepwise, ornamental figures of the kind shown in Ex. 40, bars 1, 3, 4, and 6, and Ex. 41, bars 2 and 4, must be introduced.

Dance music provides many opportunities for this sort of extemporization, but divisions should always be in keeping with the style of the dance in question; for instance, a pavan must still sound stately even when the note-values are short. And it would be wise to keep in mind the warning in Rognoni's *Selva di varii pasaggi* (1620): 'it is far better to play one note gracefully with a smooth, sweet bow stroke than to make many divisions in unsuitable places.'

In courants, as with galliards, it is most important to bring out the cross-rhythms between parts. Sometimes the rhythms are very ambiguous, as in Ex. 42, Jenkins's *Coranto*, which is shown in its original, unbarred form. If you analyse where the strong beats fall, you will find that no regular barring accommodates the pattern of stresses, although various groupings of three seem clear, and normally longer notes need more stress than shorter ones. When you

Ex. 42. Jenkins, *Coranto*

play from a barred part, try to avoid routinely accenting short notes that are 'on the beat', as this often indicates a displacement of stress on to the nearest longer note.

Some courants, such as those by Matthew Locke, sound better played with a shortened upbeat into the first bar. This often causes bowing problems in repeats since the long note at the end of the section brings you to the wrong end of the bow. The easiest solution is to end the section on a back bow and then tuck the shortened upbeat backwards as well.

English sarabands, like the one by Locke in Ex. 43, should be fairly fast and light, in contrast to French *sarabandes*, which are slow and stately. They usually feature the rhythm ♩ ♩. ♪ which demands a slight stress on both first and second notes. This may be better bowed ⊓ v ⊓ than v ⊓ v . When the rhythm occurs in sequence, v ⊓ ⊓ is a possible bowing.

Ex. 43 is very hard to bow. Try to work out all the possible alternatives and see which feels and sounds best, bringing out the cross-rhythms in the last three bars.

Courants and sarabands are more common in later dance music. Ornaments such as trills are increasingly used, normally beginning on the written note. They should be fast and light.

Ex. 43. Locke, Sarabande from Suite in D

## Fantasies

Fantasies are usually freely composed pieces based on a number of themes which are passed from one part to another. They often fall into distinct sections, though this is not always apparent on a first play-through. In general, themes are introduced one at a time; less often two are heard simultaneously. Each part will have at least one of the main themes, and these should be brought out as clearly as possible.

If you are working in depth on a piece, it is helpful to mark the appearances of thematic material, even if only fragmentary, since otherwise entries can get lost. Note that entries are often disguised by small variations, such as the lengthening or shortening of the first note of the theme.

Watch out for cadences, however short, and make sure that they are not accented, particularly when the next theme starts immediately. It is important that a new subject should be firmly registered on the listener's mind. Sometimes it is enough to do this by shortening the last note before the new theme, but do not be afraid to take extra time, so as to allow the music to breathe.

Try to give each section a distinct character: make it strong, smooth, dance-like, soft and mysterious, or whatever seems appropriate to the music. To bring out the phrasing, make sure that every note has some direction, either leading to a following note or dying away from a previous one. Where you have a melodic figure, do not release pressure on every note or you will lose any sense of line. Think of each phrase as having a shape, such as one of those illustrated in Fig. 13. As in dance music, try to think in the longest possible beats.

Bowing in fantasies can present difficulties, since it is impossible to have the bow going the right way all the time. If it corrects itself within a few notes, the passage is best bowed as it comes. If the bowing is going to be wrong for any length of time—for example, a run of quavers starting on a back bow—try to make a correction before this point is reached by tucking in a suitable place, as described below.

Fit tucks in between phrases when possible, or between a longer note and a shorter one, and not the other way round. Tuck on back bows if there is a choice, and try to avoid tucks altogether on fast notes and in passages that move by step.

*In nomines* are a special form of fantasy already mentioned above as being good material for beginners in consort playing. They are by no means easy to play well, however, since they usually consist of complex parts interweaving round the plainsong (cantus firmus). The other parts must allow the plainsong to be audible throughout the piece, like a thread running through from beginning to end, without obliging the player of that part to force the tone. It should not be necessary to play fortissimo in order for the *In nomine* to be heard.

If you are playing the cantus firmus, try to shape it as you would any other melody, and look out for particular notes that provide harmonic tension and relaxation in relation to the other parts. Occasionally the plainsong part may include a snatch of thematic material in imitation of the other parts. Don't fall asleep playing the long notes, otherwise you will miss your big moment!

## Consorts with other instruments

Until the seventeenth century viols were often played in 'broken consort' with wind and plucked instruments. A particular combination used by Morley in his *Consort Lessons* consisted of lute, treble viol, flute or recorder, bass viol, cittern, and bandora. In this case the lute was the solo instrument and played florid divisions at the repeats. *Lachrimae*, Dowland's famous set of seven pavans, was written for lute and five viols.

Nowadays a broken consort is most likely to include recorders and a variety of other wind instruments such as crumhorns, cornamuses, curtals, rackets, cornetts, or sackbuts. These work well in much sixteenth-century music and later dance movements such as those by Holborne but are less suited to fantasies.

As wind instruments have a much smaller range than viols, this will usually dictate who plays which line. But bear in mind that recorders play an octave higher than written, so avoid putting viols on lower parts if the bass part is to be played on a recorder. In general it sounds best to have the bass part at real (8 foot) pitch on bass viol, curtal, or sackbut, and let recorder players take the upper parts, but there is plenty of scope for experimentation.

## Consort songs, madrigals, and lute songs

Many of the numerous collections of madrigals published in seventeenth-century England are recommended on their title pages as being 'apt for viols or voices'. This means that almost any English madrigal, and for that matter the majority of Italian madrigals, French chansons, or any other vocal ensemble piece can be played on viols to very good effect. Such pieces can also be played with a mixture of voices and viols, with or without doubling, depending on the performers available. Byrd took this possibility further by writing consort songs specifically for one or two solo voices (usually, but not always, in the upper parts) and three, four, or five viols. In consort songs the instrumental parts have no words, whereas in the madrigals all parts have words underlaid.

In all vocal music of this period the words are the foundation of the piece and must therefore be heard. The madrigal is the vocal equivalent of the viol fantasy in that all the parts are equal, but when playing with voices one must allow the words to take precedence. This is not to say that your playing should be reticent: play strongly enough to provide support for the singers without obscuring the words. The precise volume will of course depend on the singer's voice and diction and the acoustic.

Unfortunately, few instrumental parts for consort songs and madrigals are published, so you may have to copy out parts from the vocal score. Make a point of writing in the words under the instrumental lines, since they will make the phrasing clearer. It is essential to follow this phrasing exactly, emphasizing the most important words and being careful not to accent insignificant words or syllables. Try to 'play' the words, taking account of hard and soft consonants, and bow very smoothly between two syllables of the same word. If the words are in a language you do not understand, ask the singer what they mean and how they should be stressed. It will occasionally be necessary to contradict the phrasing implied by the words in the lower parts to make the phrasing in the solo voice clear. And you may sometimes need to phrase in a way that would not be expected from the musical line in order to accommodate the words.

In consort songs, where the instrumental parts have no words, you are more free to play your line 'instrumentally'; but you are still likely to have many phrases in imitation of the voice, and at such points you should note the words and copy the singer exactly. Occasionally, the instruments will anticipate a phrase later to be sung, and in that case you need to know in advance how the singer intends to treat it.

Playing with singers encourages you to listen and respond to other members of the group and is very good for your consort playing in general. Try to apply the same principles when you next play an instrumental fantasy. You could even think of words to fit certain phrases or imagine that the piece is describing a scene or sequence of events.

All the above points apply equally to songs in which the lute takes the middle parts between voice and bass viol, as it does in many songs by Dowland,

Campion, Morley, and Ford. Dowland wrote a large number of songs which can be performed in consort settings with voices and/or viols, or alternatively as solo songs with lute and bass viol. Historically, this illustrates the beginning of a shift in emphasis from equality of voices towards a greater prominence of top and bottom. This new polarity is explored in the next section.

## 3.3. Continuo Playing

*The viol as a continuo instrument*

The seventeenth century brought about a gradual stylistic transition from the polyphony of the sixteenth century, where all the parts were more or less equal, to the Baroque style of the eighteenth, where most music was for solo voices or instruments with basso continuo. Here the composer provided a bass line with figured harmonies which could be played by any combination of keyboard, lute, theorbo, cello, bass viol, and bassoon.

The bass viol is an ideal instrument for playing continuo bass lines, as it has a very clear sound that gives plenty of support to the solo parts without drowning them or making the texture too thick. Although some composers such as Handel and Corelli use harmonic or chordal figurations that are much easier to play on the cello, and occasionally write in awkward keys such as E major, the bass line rarely requires very advanced technical ability. The viol is particularly well suited to playing continuo in French music, where a rather light sound is usually desirable.

Many people regard continuo playing as the easy alternative to solo playing, but to play continuo really well is by no means simple. However the fact that, with some exceptions, the notes themselves are usually fairly easy means that it is a good way to approach the solo repertoire. For example, even beginners can manage the Italian grounds at the end of Ortiz's book on divisions, although the divisions themselves are often extremely florid. Many of the lute songs mentioned in Section 3.2 also have very simple bass lines.

*Style and articulation*

When you play continuo for another instrument or for a singer, you should not regard your function as being merely to provide a background to the solo part.

## 3.3. Continuo Playing

You should think of yourself as an equal member of the ensemble and bring as much interest to your part as if it were the solo line.

The primary task of the continuo player is to emphasize the harmonic structure of the piece. This means giving extra weight to changes of harmony—particularly where a change is unexpected—and, correspondingly, lightening passing notes and notes that arpeggiate a single chord. In Baroque duple-time movements, the harmony tends to change at each main beat. The bass part often moves continuously in groups of four notes, as in Ex. 44, from Handel's Sonata in G minor; in such passages it usually sounds best to start each group with a long note and shorten the others progressively.

Ex. 44. Handel, Sonata in G minor, Op. 1, Larghetto

Do not stress too many beats in a bar. Indeed, in fast movements it is often only alternate bars that need stressing. Look for points of harmonic tension, and relax into the cadences. A perfect cadence is by its nature expected, and therefore needs no underlining, particularly when the next phrase starts immediately afterwards.

Try to play with plenty of articulation, but not too thick a sound, as this can obscure the solo line. Even slow movements rarely need to be played entirely legato. As a general rule, try to play anything that is melodic or moves by step fairly smoothly and shorten leaping notes, particularly before cadences. Do not use sharp accents to stress a note, but lean on the note as you begin to play. Now apply these principles to Ex. 44.

Many continuo parts intended for cello use bottom C, and the French repertoire also often includes notes going down to the A below that, making it clear that the part in question was written for a seven-string viol. If you only have six strings, it is easy to adapt such parts by jumping up an octave at the most musically satisfactory place. When there are two notes an octave apart, it is usually better to put both up an octave rather than play the same note twice.

## 3.3. Continuo Playing 95

Alternatively, if C is the lowest note, you can tune the D string down to C as is required by some English consort music.

Where there is a very florid bass part, it is often effective for one instrument—either the viol or the harpsichord—to play a simplified version that clarifies the harmonies. Which instrument this should be depends on the ability of the players, though when possible it usually sounds better for the viol to take the fast-moving part. Clearly continuo passages like the Allegro from Handel's Sonata in A Minor (Ex. 45) require as much practice and expertise as a demanding solo.

*Fingering and bowing*

Continuo parts often raise special technical problems. Since the most important role of the continuo is to clarify the harmony, it is vital that in broken-chord passages all the notes are held for the chord's duration, which may be four notes

Ex. 45. Handel, Sonata in A minor, Op. 1, Allegro

or more. The large number of leaps in such passages means that legato bowing would sound ridiculous even where it might be possible, but if a legato fingering is used the resonance of each note can continue to the next, giving a good sense of line or direction without heaviness.

Try to develop a bow stroke that has plenty of life and resonance but not too much body, except when extra weight is needed (as, for example, on unexpected changes of harmony or dissonances with the upper part). On octave leaps, make sure that the first note is substantially stronger than the second, whether the leap is up or down, and try to play the second note very clearly but absolutely without accent—it must sound like a rebound of the bow.

Try to make corrections to the bowing so that most of the strong beats come forward ( v ). In triple time this may necessitate bowings such as   v ⊓ ⊓   . Bear in mind, however, that not every bar is equally strong, and this sort of bowing should not be necessary if there is a sequence of three or five notes to a bar.

If you can read figured bass, try to work out a few simple chords to play. These will mostly consist of thirds, fifths, or sixths above the bass. It is perfectly possible to play enough harmonies for the harpsichord to become unnecessary—and to be able to do so is an especially useful accomplishment if you do not always have access to a keyboard instrument.

## Accompanying the voice

There are a few special points to consider when accompanying a singer or group of singers. As with consort songs and madrigals, be careful not to obscure the words by playing too heavily, even though many voices will need quite a strong sound to support them. Mark in the points where the singer wants to breathe (this may not always seem logical in your part). In sections where the singer is resting, you may play out strongly, but be prepared to reduce your volume at the next entry of the voice. As in the case of vocal music rendered partly or wholly on instruments (see Section 3.2 above), it is important that your style of playing should reflect the mood of the text. In Ex. 46, from Purcell's *Music for a While*, the first statement of the ground bass is given to the viol alone, with the voice entering over the second statement. The ground is repeated many more times, and you will have to play it in a variety of ways to suit the vocal line.

Playing for recitative is another very important aspect of continuo playing. Do not be deceived by the apparent simplicity of the bass line, which quite often appears as an unbroken succession of long notes. Make sure that you have at least the words, and preferably the whole of the vocal line, laid out above the viol part. You will probably find that the vocal part is very freely sung, and it is therefore

Ex. 46. Purcell, *Music for a while*

absolutely essential to follow every note. It is not always necessary or desirable to give each note its full value; some can be played quite short (though you will have to agree on the length of notes if there is more than one continuo player). While the harmonic structure is filled out by the keyboard player, the bass viol can shape the notes of the bass line, perhaps swelling towards dissonances, and generally providing a variety of tone colours to suit the meaning of the words. Once again, it is essential to understand the text. In florid recitative, the viol can often enhance the effect of the vocal line by making strong, dramatic contrasts.

## 3.4. Divisions and Duets

*Italian divisions*

A number of the extant treatises on viol playing date from the sixteenth and seventeenth centuries, and several of these include sections on how to play 'divisions', that is, the decoration of a slow-moving line with faster notes. Ganassi, Ortiz, and Rognoni all provide models of improvising on a given bass line, tune, or madrigal, as well as examples of free extemporization. Of these, the models given by Ortiz are probably the most straightforward.

Ortiz's book is in two parts. The first gives many examples of how to decorate cadences and introduce divisions between two notes. The second part gives extended examples of divisions of many different types. Two pieces based on vocal compositions, *O felici occhi miei* and *Doulce Memoire*, include ornamentations of the treble line in a high register, and can therefore be played on the treble or tenor viol, though Ortiz himself says that all of the pieces sound best on bass.

The final section of the Second Part contains nine sets of divisions in the bass range on Italian grounds. The excitement of these pieces lies partly in the complete rhythmic independence that the divisions have from the regularity of the ground. Think in as long a pulse as possible, as this gives you more freedom to play the divisions without sounding too rigid.

Ganassi and Rognoni also wrote extensively on how to play divisions and give many examples of ways in which cadences can be decorated. Ganassi includes a few *recercadas*, freely composed, which go very high and can also be played on smaller instruments. Rognoni, and other composers such as Dalla Casa, Virgiliano, Bassano, and Selma, wrote many sets of divisions on madrigals and chansons, as well as freely composed, unaccompanied *recercadas*. Some are for unspecified treble instrument (but can also be played on the tenor viol an octave lower). Other pieces are in the style known as *viola bastarda*, meaning that the viol plays a 'bastard' part, taking melodic fragments from all voices of the original madrigal or chanson, and also making additions. These pieces often cover a very large range, which may indicate the use of a wider tuning than normal, perhaps in fifths and fourths. Many are extremely virtuosic. Rognoni writes in three ways, which he calls easy, moderate, and difficult, but even his 'easy' pieces make considerable technical demands.

## English divisions

Simpson's divisions are much later in style and altogether more 'instrumental' than the Italian divisions. At the end of his book *The Division Viol* are three preludes and eight sets of divisions, arranged in approximate order of difficulty. Earlier there are instructions on how to hold the viol and bow and some exercises. Extracts from these and from the divisions are given in Exx. 47–50.

Simpson gives a rule for holding on the fingers, stating that, after you have used a finger, you should hold it down 'until some occasion require the taking it off'. The square brackets in Ex. 47 indicate the holds shown by Simpson; the fingering is also his. This exercise can be played at any speed, depending on ability, and provides extremely good practice for fingers and bow.

Unlike the Italian composers, Simpson often included extended chordal passages in his sets of divisions. In the first part of his book he gives a series of chordal progressions increasing very rapidly in difficulty. Ex. 48 is the first. The fingerings are all Simpson's; notice how he uses all the fingers to minimize jumping from chord to chord.

3.4. *Divisions and Duets* 99

Ex. 47. Simpson, Exercise for holding fingers

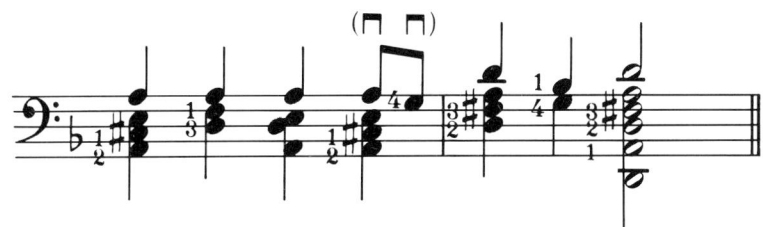

Ex. 48. Simpson, Chord exercises

One of Simpson's less difficult pieces is the Prelude in D major, from his 'Divisions for the Practice of Learners' (Ex. 49.). (That is not to say that it is easy, but the last piece in the book is almost unplayable.) Use should be made of chordal fingerings to avoid any jumping, except at the start of bar 7, which is further than most people can stretch. In this case the fingering suggested is not original—Simpson only gives fingerings in his preliminary exercises.

In this piece starting backwards would be the obvious bowing, but this would mean using a different bowing for the similar phrase in bar 3. It is preferable to

Ex. 49. Simpson, Prelude in D major

use a bowing that will work in both places, as suggested. The shift in bar 3 is best done between the two repeated notes, since a small musical comma is desirable at that point. Phrase the first bar in the same way. The complete Prelude is shown in facsimile in Fig. 24.

Simpson's Divisions in E minor (Ex. 50) are possibly his finest. One of the many problems they present to the player is how to bow the dotted notes. Ideally they should come on the forward bow; where this is not possible the little note should be tucked in backwards to bring the bowing right at the earliest opportunity. Frequent tucks are unavoidable in this passage, but it should be possible to make them sound identical to the bowed-out groups. Although the dotted notes which are tucked require some movement of the arm, most of the others should be done with the fingers only, and certainly not with the wrist, since this would make the dotted rhythm sound very sloppy.

3.4. Divisions and Duets   101

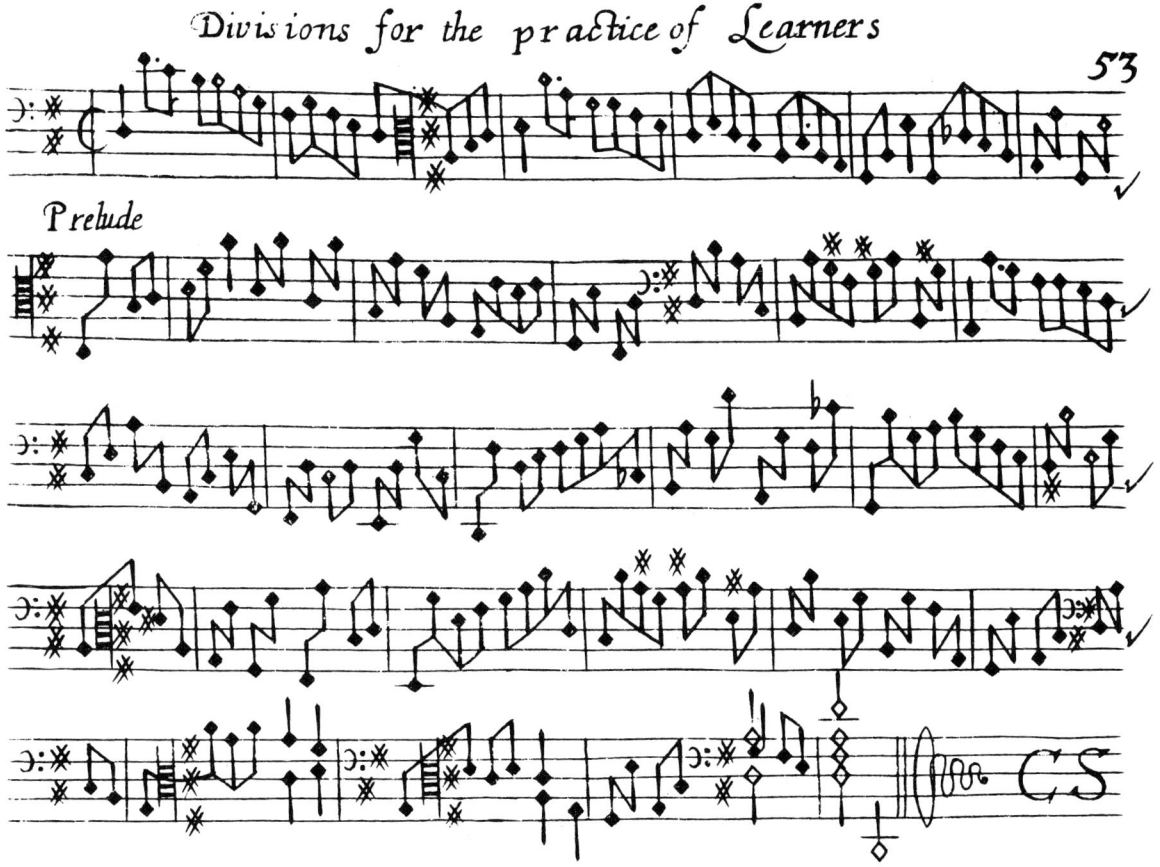

Fig. 24. Simpson, Prelude in D major (facsimile)

## Playing in high positions

The use of the high register is another technical problem in divisions. Even when Ganassi was writing in 1542, it is clear that the bass viol was often expected to play above the frets. Simpson gives one exercise which goes up to top A, right at the end of the fingerboard, and says, 'if you find difficulty . . . play it the slower, until your Hand have overcome it'. (This may take years, if not a lifetime!)

In fingering high passages it is often better to cross two or even three strings in one position rather than shift up and down the top string too many times. In very high positions it is possible to use diatonic fingering (covering a fourth), as many treble players do. Remember that you can crawl to minimize shifting (see Section 2.4). Follow normal rules for shifting when it is unavoidable, or when stopping notes very high on the lower strings makes the sound too fluffy.

102    3.4. *Divisions and Duets*

Ex. 50. Simpson, Divisions in E minor, variation 4

It is just as important to produce a beautiful sound at the very top of the viol as in the middle range, but considerably more difficult. Press your fingers down on the strings much harder than when playing on the frets, and keep the bow close to the bridge even in quiet passages.

Ex. 51 is the opening of a set of divisions of 'medium' difficulty by Rognoni. Begin on the second string and experiment with different possibilities of fingering the long run from D up to high E.

## Style in division playing

Regardless of technical difficulties, do not forget that, when you play divisions, they should sound like ornamentations of the ground, madrigal, or whatever underlying structure they are based on. It is very easy to let the embellishments obscure the melody or ground on which the piece was originally built. *Recercadas* on ground basses, such as those of Ortiz, need to be played very freely within the main pulse; for example, a run of quavers could well speed up towards the end, but the main beat must remain steady.

In later divisions, like Simpson's there are often bowed-out trills consisting of notes twice as fast as anything else in the piece. Do not judge the speed of the

Ex. 51. Rognoni, Divisions on *Vestiva i colli*

whole piece by these very fast notes; they can be played by using a minute amount of bow and letting the arm tremble while keeping the wrist relaxed.

Try to distinguish between melodic patterns (with a predominance of stepwise movement) and harmonic ones (patterns that arpeggiate a chord); in general, melodic writing demands greater legato and harmonic a more detached style of playing. Decide on the phrasing, stressing, and structure of the ground or tune and apply the same to the divisions, except where they are so freely composed that they do not follow the same pattern.

Apart from the solo divisions with a second bass viol playing the ground, there are many pieces for two division viols, including some for treble and bass, by Simpson, Jenkins, Lawes, and other, lesser-known English composers of the seventeenth century. Treble viol and violin were often regarded as interchangeable at this period, and in many cases treble parts work equally well on violin. Ensemble divisions were also written for various combinations of treble viols (or violins) and bass viols, usually with continuo. Among the most attractive of these pieces are Simpson's fantasy suites, *The Months* and *The Seasons*. Jenkins wrote similar suites as well as an exciting programmatic piece, *Newark Siege*.

## Extemporizing divisions

As already mentioned, several treatises describe in considerable detail how to extemporize divisions, but many people play all the examples in these books without ever considering that they might do the real thing themselves. This is understandable, for, as Rousseau says, improvisation needs 'more science, more inspiration and more technique than all the other ways of playing'.

The best way to start is by practising with another player, ideally someone with whom you can alternate playing ground and divisions. (A less satisfactory alternative is to record the ground yourself, repeating it many times, and play along with the tape.) Pick a very easy ground to begin with, such as *Bergamasca* in Ex. 52; the ground repeats the same harmonic pattern in every bar.

Ex. 52. Anon., *Bergamasca*

If you play treble, you may prefer to start with extemporizing on a tune rather than a ground, as you will be more familiar with melodies than bass parts. First play one or both parts many times until you know them really well. You should become aware of what other notes will fit in the harmonies without having to work them out. Try humming or singing other notes while you play the bass or treble, and then play those notes instead. The advantage of this is that it makes you pitch the note entirely by ear, whereas most people playing an instrument feel they need to know what the actual note is. A safe bet is to play a third or sometimes a fifth above the written line, filling in with passing notes as described in the section on consort music.

If you prefer a more systematic approach to improvising, follow the advice given by Simpson, who describes five ways of breaking the ground. It is a good idea to practise these separately before going on to combine two or more. The five ways are as follows:

1. Repeat the ground or its octave in notes of smaller value.
2. Move away from the first ground note, returning to it before going on to the the next one.
3. Move away from the first ground note in the direction of the next.
4. Move by leaps to notes harmonizing with the ground note.
5. Move by leaps but add passing notes to connect some of the intervals.

The next stage is descanting, using at first only the intervals of a third, fifth, sixth, and octave above the ground. To begin with keep the descant moving in notes of the same value as the ground notes. The usual rules for progression of parts apply: two or more thirds and sixths may be used in succession, but not two octaves or two fifths.

It is extremely important to keep a strong feeling of rhythm: whoever is playing the slow notes should insist on playing in time, however hesitant the other player's initial attempts may be. Once you are confident about playing one note for each note of a tune or ground that moves, say, in crotchets, add a few faster notes. Occasionally you will find yourself ending on a note which sounds completely wrong, especially as you begin to play faster and more elaborate divisions. Don't worry: if you never make mistakes it is probably a sign that you are not being sufficiently adventurous.

There is no shortage of suitable grounds: one by Jenkins is given in Ex. 53 and there are many to be found in Ortiz and Simpson. You can also extemporize on well-known tunes such as *Greensleeves* or on some of the tunes in *First Solos*, such as 'Goe from my Window'.

When you get more confident you might try decorating a madrigal. Again you will need someone to play or sing the other parts. Begin by decorating one line, and eventually move from one voice to another, ornamenting the most suitable parts of each line. Include some longer notes too, and avoid too much continuous quaver movement.

Improvising a counterpoint to a cantus firmus such as the *In nomine* plainsong or *La Spagna* is perhaps rather harder to do. Try if possible to play a line above the

Ex. 53. Jenkins, Ground

cantus firmus, again confining yourself to thirds, fifths, sixths, and octaves to start with. Gradually add some moving notes, and then try occasional suspensions.

It is a good idea to play through some of the examples in Ortiz, Ganassi, and Simpson which show how to decorate cadences, so as to enlarge your repertoire of ideas. These can then be incorporated (eventually without conscious thought) into your extemporizations.

Division extemporization in groups makes a pleasant change from consort playing, and infinite variations are possible. The simplest form is for one player to break the ground while the others play the bass line; descanting parts can be added later. The different possibilities of the chosen ground can be explored by passing the parts round in a circle, so that each person plays ground, division, and descant in succession. With practice this can produce a most satisfying musical performance.

### Duets and trios

In addition to the divisions for two bass viols already mentioned, there is a large repertoire of duets in other styles by English composers of the seventeenth century.

Collections of fantasies and airs by Ward and Coprario have organ or continuo parts, as do the more extended suites for treble (or violin) and bass by Coprario and Locke. For some of these the continuo part is essential, but there are also duets by East, Jenkins, White, Withy, and Locke written without continuo, and Gibbons, Morley, and Coprario wrote duets for trebles and tenors.

Duets often combine elements of consort, continuo, and solo playing. The two viols may be equal throughout, the two lines interweaving continuously as in a consort fantasy, or one may be providing the accompaniment for an upper part which, as in solo music, uses the high register and needs considerable projection.

In many of the bass duets the two viols are equal in range but alternate between playing the melody and the bass line every few bars, or even every few notes, as in Ex. 54, a passage from the Courante from Locke's Suite in D. It was also a common practice for the players to exchange parts on the repeats. When playing duets of this kind, look for the points where you change from melody to bass and also for imitation between the parts.

There are trios in a similar style for three bass viols by composers like John Hingeston and Benjamin Hely, as well as other duets and trios for varying combinations of treble and bass instruments, with and without continuo. Duets

Ex. 54. Locke, Courante from Suite in D

and trios for bass viols continued to be very popular well into the eighteenth century (see Section 3.6).

## 3.5. Lyra Viol

Although the term 'lyra viol' was sometimes applied to a particular size of instrument half-way between tenor and bass, it more usually refers to a style of playing, sometimes called 'lyra way'. In this style the music is mainly chordal in character and is written in a tablature similar to that used for lute music. Because of the complexity of some of the chords, it is often easier to play lyra music on a smaller viol, as long as the body is big enough to produce plenty of sound. Thus this music is very useful to tenor players, who do not have a solo repertoire of their own.

## 3.5. Lyra Viol

### The lyra-viol repertoire

There is a large amount of music for solo lyra viol, mostly by English composers, though Le Sieur de Machy in France wrote some pieces in tablature. Playford's 1682 collection, prefaced by 'Brief Rules and Instructions for young Practitioners', includes seventy-seven pieces in order of difficulty, which he describes as 'short and easie'. Fig. 25 shows an Almain from this book, *Musick's Recreation on the Viol, Lyra Way*, in facsimile.

An earlier and prolific composer for the lyra viol was Captain Tobias Hume. The prefaces to his collections are written in his own highly individual style—to commend music, he says, 'were but to reach the Sunne a paire of spectacles'—and his pieces have evocative titles: *Tickle me Quickly, A Snatch and Away, This Sport is Ended*. Some are for two or three lyra viols. Hume's works, as well as those of Ford, Ferrabosco, Lawes, Corkine, Coprario, and others, are mostly available in facsimile.

There are also a number of recent modern editions, which are perhaps less daunting in the early stages of reading tablature, and they have the further advantage that the not infrequent mistakes in the originals are corrected.

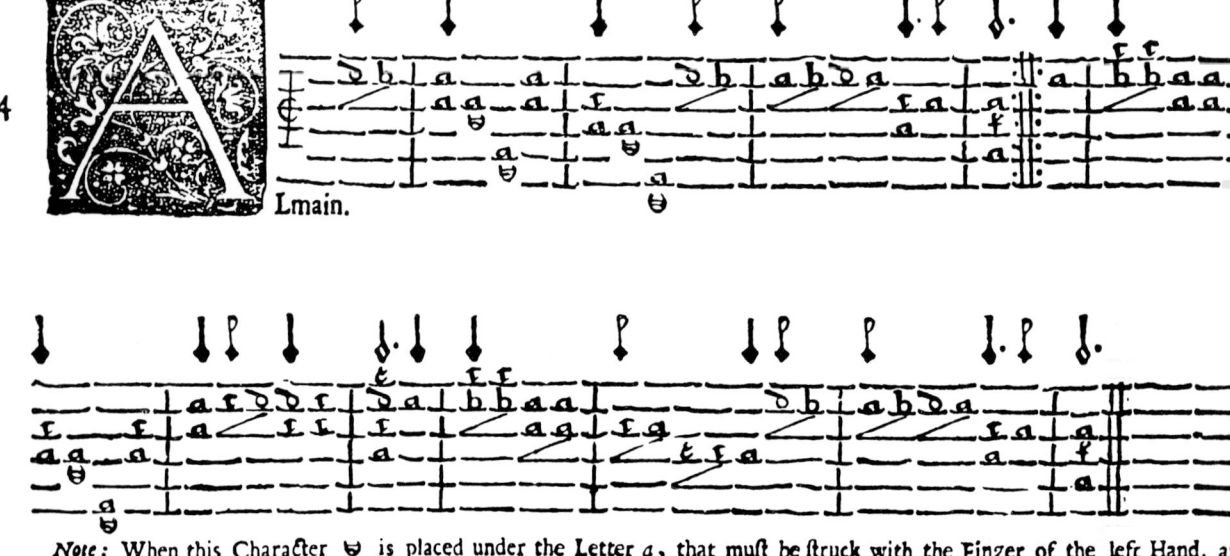

Fig. 25. Playford, *Musick's Recreation on the Viol, Lyra Way*, Almain (facsimile)

## 3.5. Lyra Viol

In some editions pieces are printed with transcriptions in staff notation. This helps the player to see the shape of the music, which is very difficult to do in tablature. But it is a pity not to make the effort to learn to read tablature, as this brings so much attractive music within reach. At the first few attempts it may feel as if you are going right back to the beginning, because both left and right hand are having to respond to unfamiliar symbols. Many people give up at that point, but if you persevere you will find that it rapidly becomes easier.

It is especially worth mastering tablature if you live too far from other viol players to have regular opportunities to play in ensembles. The harmony in lyra music being self-contained, it needs no accompaniment, and is entirely satisfying to play alone.

### Reading tablature

Most lyra music is in French tablature. The six lines represent the six strings (seven strings are never used), with the highest at the top. Letters, placed above the appropriate line, show the fret to be stopped on each string. The letter *a* represents an open string, *b* the first fret, *c* the second, and so on (NB Playford's 'e' looks similar to a modern 't'). Ex. 55, from Sumarte's *Daphne*, shows a simple piece of tablature (Ex. 55a) together with a transcription for tenor viol in G (Ex. 55b).

The flag above the letter indicates the rhythm as in ordinary notation, except that it is not repeated for successive notes of the same value. So one flag, for example ♪, indicates that you should keep playing quavers until something

Ex. 55. Sumarte, *Daphne*, tablature and transcription

## 3.5. Lyra Viol

different is indicated. Rests are shown by a flag with no corresponding fret letters. A stroke under two or more notes means a slur. A special feature of lyra-viol music is the 'thump', which means a left-hand pizzicato; this is indicated by a dot below a note, or a special sign, as in Fig. 25.

### Lyra-viol tunings

One of the reasons why lyra music uses tablature is that this makes possible a variety of different tunings without creating difficulties for the player. Since at one time there were around fifty recognized tunings for the lyra viol, it is easy to see how essential this was.

The tunings are designed to make it easy to play chords and give increased resonance through the use of more fifths and octaves. Unisons frequently occur, obtained by playing on two strings at once, one open and one stopped.

Chords are much simpler to read and play from tablature. The system of notation is a very direct one that shows you where to put your fingers. In this respect it is more exact than staff notation, since it specifies precisely where each note is to be played: open or stopped, and on which string.

The tuning for a piece is indicated by fret letters. Stop the stated fret on the lower of two strings and tune the lower string in unison with the upper. Thus normal viol tuning would be written *ffeff*.

The composer could choose a tuning to suit a particular piece and key. The most popular tunings are shown below:

| | |
|---|---|
| Viol or plain tuning | *ffeff* |
| Viol tuning with low C | *ffefh* |
| Lyra way, or Bandora sette | *fefhf* |
| Harpway sharp | *defhf* |
| High harpway sharp | *fdefh* |
| Harpway flat | *edfhf* |
| High harpway flat | *fedfh* |
| Eights | *fhfhf* |
| Alfonso way | *ffhfh* |

Playford suggests that you begin to tune by raising or 'screwing up' the first string 'as high as it will conveniently bear without breaking, then Tune the other to it'. Miscalculations can be expensive with this method, however, and most modern players would prefer to drop the overall pitch rather than put a strain on the upper strings.

## *'In imitation of the lute'*

Lyra-viol style was, according to Playford, 'a late invention in imitation of the Old English Lute or Bandora'. The viol has an advantage over the lute in being able to play a melody legato, although it is more limited as a polyphonic instrument. If you play lyra way, you are playing both tune and accompaniment, and it is important to identify which notes are part of the melody and which of the accompaniment, or counterpoint.

In chords the melody may be at the top, bottom, or middle, and the biggest difficulty is to bring out the important notes so that the part-writing can be heard. This can be helped by varying the speed of spread of the chord, and allowing longer time or more tone on the important note (see Section 2.3 for general advice on playing chords). Beware of playing accompanying notes too heavily. A sequence of notes that are part of the same harmony usually only need the first note to be stressed. Try not to 'scrunch' on every chord, otherwise the piece will sound very disjointed. Practise playing just the melody, without any chords, and gradually add the harmonies without disturbing the flow of the tune. Also practise plucking (as on a lute) and strumming the chords gently with the thumb.

Occasionally there may be a sequence of chords that sound better with all three or four notes played simultaneously (this is especially good for a martial effect). In this case play further from the bridge and use a faster bow speed; this does not necessarily mean using a lot of bow, as the bow can be lifted off the string immediately after the chord is sounded.

In general, lyra-viol music should be played with airy, resonant bow strokes, emulating the sound of the lute. Try to release the pressure very quickly, as this will allow the natural resonances of the instrument, enhanced by the tunings, to be heard to full effect.

## *Fingering*

Fingerings for lyra-viol music can be quite difficult to work out, as it is very important to minimize the need for fingers to jump from one note to another (see Sections 1.4 and 2.4). The hand often needs to be bunched up, with all the fingers very close together. Do not avoid the use of the fourth finger, as this can make a vast difference to the possibilities of resonance.

Look at the fret letters. Where they are mostly *b*, *c*, and *d* this indicates a contracted half position with first finger on *b*, fourth finger on *d*, and others

Ex. 56. Hume, I am Falling

moving around as necessary. A piece in which *b* does not occur would be played entirely in first position or higher. Try to hold any fingers which play melody notes while accompanying notes are played on lower strings. An example of fingering is shown in Ex. 56, from Hume's *I am Falling*. This piece should be played entirely in contracted half position. Use of the fingering indicated will eliminate almost completely any need to jump from chord to chord.

## 3.6. Sonatas, Arias, and Chamber Music

There are many late seventeenth- or early eighteenth-century sonatas for one viol (sometimes two or three), with or without continuo; some have obbligato parts for harpsichord. They are mostly by composers of German or Austrian origin, such as J. S. Bach, Telemann, Handel, Schenk, Kuhnel, Finger, Abel, and C. P. E. Bach.

There is also chamber music featuring obbligato viol parts. This includes a set of trio sonatas by Buxtehude for violin, viol, and continuo, and several trio sonatas by Telemann for various combinations of instruments (including some for treble viol). Telemann also wrote twelve 'Paris' quartets for flute, violin, bass viol or cello, and continuo.

One of the biggest difficulties in playing sonatas from the Baroque period is the question of slurring. Unfortunately, many modern editions have heavily edited viol parts that often suggest bowings and fingerings more suited to the cello and add numerous slurs not in the text. Look at a facsimile reproduction if you can to see which slurs, if any, were specified by the composer. You can then make your own judgement about those which could be mistakes in copying, for instance when two identical phrases are slurred differently for no apparent reason. Slurring in the Bach sonatas is especially problematic, due to discrepancies in the original sources, but there are now several good editions

## 3.6. Sonatas, Arias, and Chamber Music 113

which offer various plausible readings. If a facsimile is not easily available, look at the viol part in the keyboard score, as this is often Urtext and gives only the original markings.

On the whole German composers did not bother to make the bowing work out in every bar, so you will have to make tucks in the bowing in various places and possibly add, or take out, a few slurs to make it work. Ornaments are often indicated by a small cross, or left out altogether, so add trills at cadence points, and perhaps more elaborate decorations on repeats. On the other hand, watch out for editions where too much ornamentation has been added, and again check with the original where possible. In trio sonatas make sure that both solo parts match their slurring in parallel phrases, and work out ornaments together.

### Telemann

Telemann wrote several solo sonatas for viol, including an unaccompanied one in D major and a G major sonata originally for treble viol. Most are available both in facsimile and in modern editions. The Sonata in A minor is the easiest to start with, but there are a few awkward fingerings, as in the passage shown in Ex. 57. Although it may be harder than shifting halfway down, this crawling fingering gives a much smoother result.

Ex. 57. Telemann, Sonata in A minor, Allegro

In the E minor Sonata the bowing and fingering of the opening (Ex. 58) both present problems. The bowing indicated may seem fussy, but there are good reasons for suggesting it. If you start with a back bow, which might seem the obvious way, it is not possible to repeat the bowing for the similar phrase in bar 5 because of the run of semiquavers beforehand. It is also better to get the last two notes of the phrase sounding strong–weak, that is bowed forward–back.

The shift works very well in the same place as the tuck since there will be a small gap at that point. It also means moving after the longest note and, in the first case, only requires a semitone shift. However the fourth is not the easiest finger to shift on, and the real difficulty lies in getting it to sound as if there is no shift or tuck between the second and third notes, since the whole phrase should be legato.

Ex. 58. Telemann, Sonata in E minor, Cantabile

The two extracts in Ex. 59 show the extremes to which chordal fingering can (and should) be taken in order to obtain maximum resonance in harmonic patterns. In both examples the harmony will only continue to sound if the finger on the first note of each bar is held for the whole bar. In Ex. 59a second and third fingers can be interchanged, depending on which you find least difficult. In bars 3, 4, and 5 of Ex. 59b the substitution of a different finger on the last note of the bar means that it is easier to get the correct finger down at the beginning of the following bar.

The bowing pattern in this movement is nearly always . Because this goes on for so long it is important not to travel down the bow but to keep near the tip.

Ex. 59. Telemann, Sonata in E minor, Allegro (2nd movement)

## J. S. Bach

Bach's three sonatas for viol and obbligato harpsichord are among the finest pieces in the repertoire. The first, in G major, is perhaps the easiest, and the third, in G minor, by far the hardest. Exx. 60–2 illustrate some specific problems that appear in the sonatas.

In Ex. 60 there is a sequence of long slurs. Where possible they should be fingered with the same pattern each time as suggested. Note that the shifts come between phrases and that no attempt should be made to shift within a slur, except by extensions and contractions. Move down the bow as far as possible on the long note before the slur, but not so far that you cannot change bow properly. Avoid accenting the first note of the long slur in your efforts to change direction.

Ex. 61 shows probably the hardest passage in the whole of the D major Sonata. It is certainly the fastest, and includes some rather awkward slurs. When, as here, it is necessary to slur on to a strong beat, use the middle finger on the bow hair to give the extra stress needed, but do not be tempted to use more bow, as this will make the rhythm less clear. In general, passages that include a lot of string crossing need less bow than those on one or two adjacent strings. Find a fingering which does not require any shifting within the slurs except by crawling.

116   3.6. Sonatas, Arias, and Chamber Music

Ex. 60. Bach, Sonata in G major, Allegro

The opening of the Sonata in G minor (Ex. 62) is reminiscent of Brandenburg Concerto No. 3. The problem here is not so much the notes, which are easy compared with later passages, but in making good sense of the rhythm. This is extremely repetitive and it is important not to over-accent, which will give a static feeling with no sense of line. Aim for long phrases with a very clear direction. For practice, try playing the rhythm on one note while imagining the melody, and work out the hierarchy of stress for each note and its purpose in the phrase.

The following general advice may also be helpful when you work on these pieces. Unlike many German composers, Bach notates his ornaments very carefully, so play them exactly as written, but do not allow them to become too important, especially when they occur on weak beats. In the fast movements it is essential to vary the articulation for the different patterns, which are often repeated many times, otherwise the music will sound like a sewing machine. You need to agree with the harpsichordist about this, as all these pieces are really trio sonatas, with the right hand of the harpsichord paired with the viol over the left hand's bass. Look at a score and try to see where the different themes take over in each part.

The slow movements of Bach's sonatas present quite different problems from the faster ones. Many passages require extremely long notes to be played in one

## 3.6. Sonatas, Arias, and Chamber Music 117

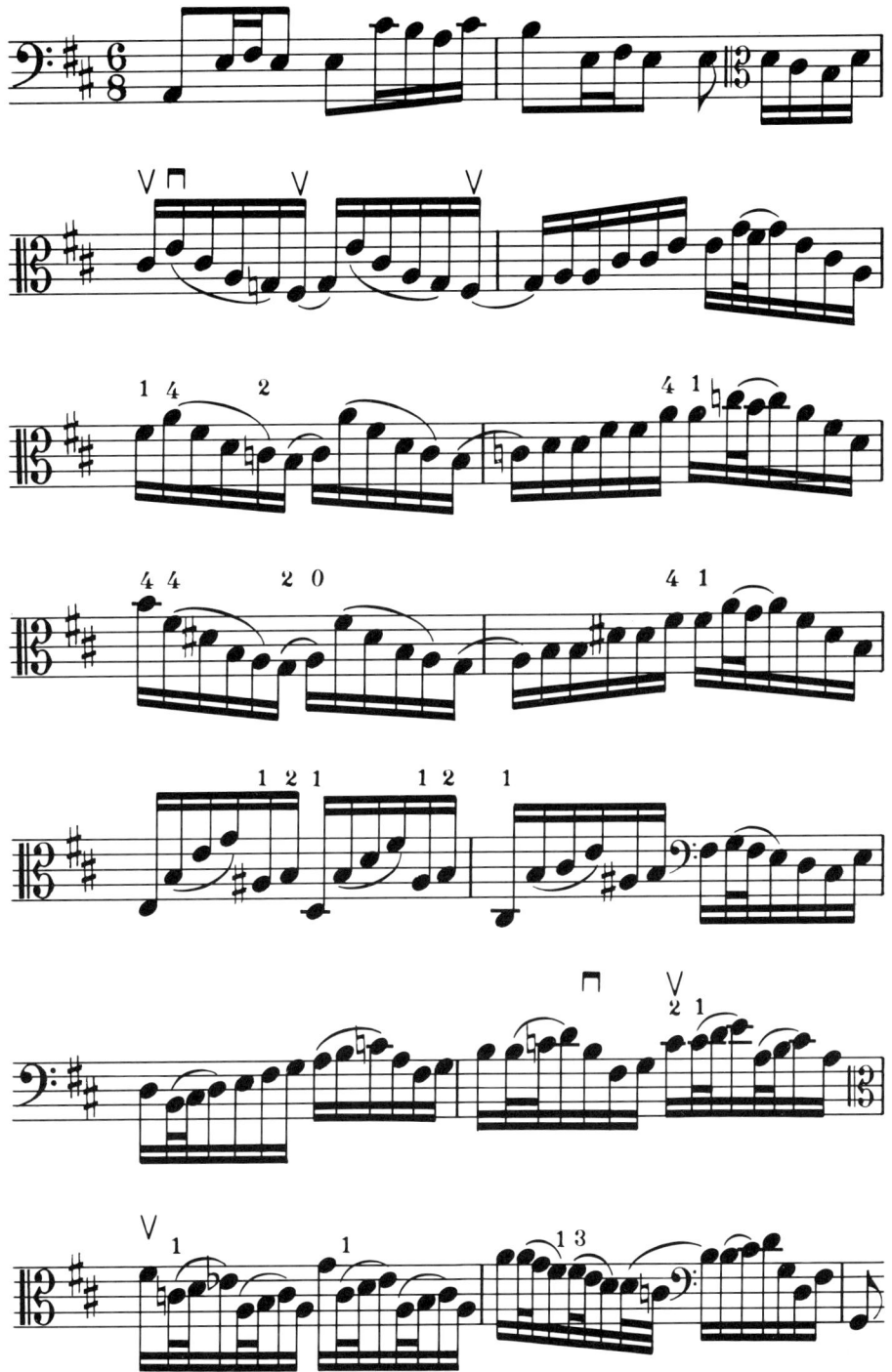

Ex. 61. Bach, Sonata in D major, Allegro (4th movement)

118  3.6. Sonatas, Arias, and Chamber Music

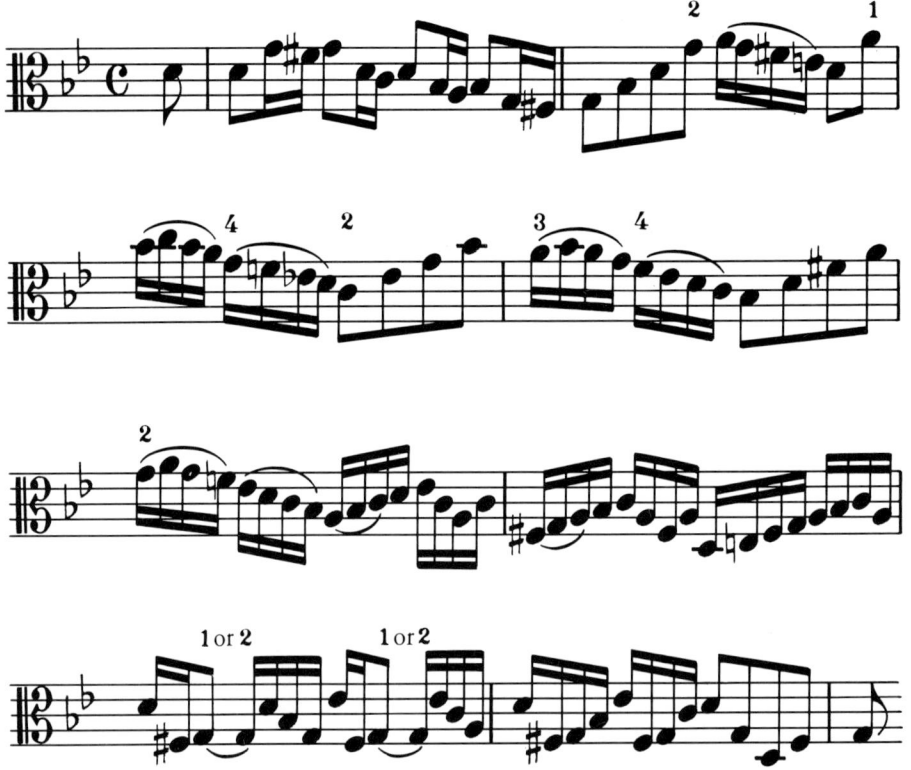

Ex. 62. Bach, Sonata in G minor, Vivace

bow and are often followed by much faster decorative ones. Practise the long notes even more slowly than you will have to play them and also using less bow, so that when the time comes to play them in context they will seem comparatively easy. Practise varying the sound, using suitable combinations of pressure and distance from the bridge, and also vary the bow speed, which helps to give direction to a phrase.

Many of the fast notes in these movements are really written-out ornaments. Try to identify these and play them appropriately. It helps to break down the line into its most simple form; play this several times without decoration so that you can keep it in mind when playing the decorated version.

In movements with very long bars, for instance in 12/8 time, do not divide up the beat into too many small parts. Think of four dotted crotchet beats, of which the first and third are stronger than the second and fourth, except where changes of harmony occur. Make sure that you are aware of the harmonic structure of the movement and know when your tied or suspended notes are dissonant or consonant with the harpsichord part.

Apart from the three gamba sonatas, Bach also wrote some beautiful obbligatos in the cantatas and passions, and parts for two bass viols in Brandenburg Concerto No. 6. The *St Matthew Passion* includes two arias for solo voice with viola da gamba obbligato, of which the second, 'Komm, süsses Kreuz', is particularly difficult but well worth practising. There is also a very moving aria, 'Es ist vollbracht', with a rather easier part for bass viol in the *St John Passion*. The cantatas No. 106 (*Actus tragicus*) and No. 198 (*Trauer ode*) both include extensive solo parts for viol.

## Other composers

One of the last composers to write for the viol was C. F. Abel (1723–87). He was himself a virtuoso player, which is probably why some of his unaccompanied music is so difficult. He did, however, write over seventy sonatas with continuo, many of which do not present any great technical problems. A few are published with alternative clefs and can equally well be played on treble.

The unaccompanied Sonata in G major, from which Ex. 63 is taken, is well within the capacity of intermediate viol players. It is a tuneful piece, fun to play and with lots of audience appeal. Use a combination of barred and contracted fingerings to get the smoothest change from chord to chord (see Section 2.4) and remember not to press any harder than usual with the bow. Playing the anticipatory d' before the final chord allows time to put the fingers down.

Abel's unaccompanied Prelude in D minor (Ex. 64) provides a wonderful study in arpeggios. Abel gives examples of the patterns of arpeggiation he intends and then expects the player to continue the pattern from the chords that follow.

Ex. 63. Abel, Sonata in G major, Adagio

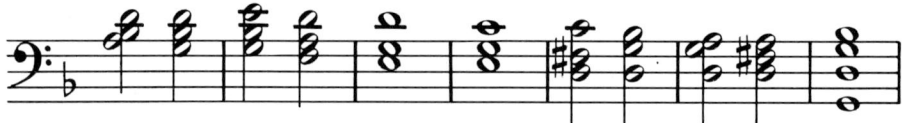

Ex. 64. Abel, Prelude in D minor

For slurred patterns like these it is important to get a very regular movement of the bow so that you are able to make the notes even in length and stress. Only when you have the control to do this should you lengthen some notes and put more stress on others. Each change of harmony should be slightly pointed, but aim to give the more 'tense' chords greater stress than the 'relaxed' ones. Also take care that the changes of pattern (for example from six notes to four) do not sound too abrupt. Work out a fingering that keeps jumping between chords to a minimum, and practise passages first chordally and then arpeggiated.

Johannes Schenk (1660–c.1712) might be thought of as the Austrian counterpart to Marais, in that he too is almost unknown except as a composer for the viol. His large output includes many pieces for two viols and is very varied in style. Some of it sounds more French or Italian than German, and the sonatas often include dance movements. These are frequently preceded by preludes built up of broken chords, as in Ex. 65.

Schenk has the notes bowed out instead of slurred, which creates quite a different effect from the arpeggiated chords in the Abel prelude (Ex. 64). However they should still be fingered as if they were chords, to enhance the resonance.

There are a few modern editions of some of Schenk's suites and sonatas and an increasing number of facsimiles are becoming available.

Handel wrote a sonata in G minor which fits very well on tenor viol, though it was probably written for bass. Another sonata in C major with obbligato harpsichord is attributed to him but is almost certainly spurious. C. P. E. Bach (1714–88) wrote three sonatas that are all very late in style and technically demanding. Some rather easier sonatas survive by lesser-known composers such as Kuhnel, Benda, Erlebach, and Finger, including a number for two and three viols.

Ex. 65. Schenk, Prelude in D minor

## 3.7. French Suites

Probably more solo music for the viol was produced in France during the seventeenth and eighteenth centuries than in all other countries put together. Most of the music was composed in suites consisting of a variable number of dance movements, usually preceded by a prelude and sometimes including character pieces and fantasies.

In the earlier period, when the distinctive French style was establishing itself, the music still shows considerable influence of contemporary lute writing. De

Machy wrote some pieces in tablature similar to English lyra-viol music as well as many pieces in staff notation.

Sainte-Colombe (died c.1695) was responsible for introducing the seventh string to the viol; this sounded the bottom A a fourth below the D string, and his music makes much use of the extra low notes. He wrote a large number of suites for two bass viols without continuo. Most of these are rather difficult, especially at the cadences, where he still uses bowed-out unslurred trills, as does Simpson in his divisions. These are hard anyway, and to get them exactly together with someone else is even more difficult.

Sainte-Colombe's star pupil was Marin Marais (1656–1728), who became the most prolific viol composer of all. He wrote five large books of music, mostly for one viol and continuo but including some suites for two viols and continuo. All five are available in very clear facsimile, and some pieces have also been published in modern editions. Many of his works are quite easy and may perhaps have been written for his pupils; others are clearly intended to display the composer's own virtuosic technique. Some extracts are given as exercises below.

Other French composers who wrote solo or duet music for the viol are Caix d'Hervelois, Forqueray, Francois Couperin, Dollé, and Morel. The music of the last two is not so easily available, and then only in fascimile, but that of the others can all be found both in modern and facsimile editions. Caix d'Hervelois is probably the best composer to start with; his pieces, even when they look difficult, tend to lie easily under the hand, and are usually very tuneful. Forqueray and Couperin are considerably harder, since they use high positions and complicated chord progressions.

The pardessus, a fourth higher than the treble, was developed to extend the top range of the viol as the seven-string bass did the bottom (see Section 5.1). There is a substantial repertoire of works by Caix d'Hervelois, Heudeline, and Dollé, some of them available in modern editions or in facsimile. The music can usually be played on an ordinary treble, although it goes quite high.

Marais, Couperin, and Rameau also wrote chamber music including the viol, together with violin and/or flute and harpsichord. Rameau's *Pièces de clavecin en concert* use the full range of the instrument from bottom to top A, and the composer provides an alternative second part that can be played by a second violin instead of viol. Unfortunately he wrote no solo music for viol. However it seems that French viol players of the time often played music written for other instruments. Forqueray, for example, recommended his pupils to become familiar with the 'little neck' of the instrument, i.e. the part above the frets, in order that they should be able to play 'all the most difficult things usually only played on the violin, flute and harpsichord'.

## The French style

The French masters considered their way of playing greatly superior to that of foreign composers. According to Rousseau (1687):

It is certain that the tenderness of the French style in imitating the voice is better than all those chords and diminutions of the English, whose technique is admired more than their good taste, and which is a feeble substitute for the delicacy needed for the perfection of the French style of viol playing.

What exactly characterizes this style is difficult to describe on paper. You can get an idea of it by listening to some good recordings of French music by leading players, such as Wieland Kuijken or Jordi Savall (see the Discography).

Unlike the Austro-German repertoire, most French music is notated very exactly, with bowing, fingering, and ornaments precisely indicated. The bowing is nearly always perfectly worked out, so that strong beats come on a forward bow without tucking. Fingering is given in places where it might not be obvious. Sometimes the fingerings seem rather complicated—for instance the fourth finger might be used at the third or even at the second fret—but there are always good reasons. Usually such fingerings are designed either to allow you to hold down more fingers and so increase resonance, or to help you to get into a better position for finding the notes or chords that follow.

A feature of French style is the inequality of notes. Stepwise groups of notes of equal value should often be played *inégal*, the first note of each pair slightly longer than the second. Another important aspect of inequality is that most sequences of notes should be played alternately strong–weak. It is therefore very important to feel the difference between *poussez* and *tirez* bow strokes. Try to develop the feeling of tension on the *poussez* and relaxation on the *tirez* strokes. Inequality in French music is a complex subject; for more detailed discussion, see Bol (1973), Donington (1978), and Neumann (1982).

Many of the French treatises indicate that the bow stroke should sound like the plucking of a lute. This effect is achieved by gripping the string before the note is begun and releasing the pressure immediately as the bow begins to move. This decrease of tension continues until the end of the stroke, when the bow is frequently lifted off the string. This type of stroke is only one of many that were undoubtedly used, but try to allow plenty of air between some notes, and use the resonance of the instrument to join notes rather than always keeping the bow firmly on the string.

The detailed instructions found in French music make it extremely good for learning—it is almost a tutor in itself.

## Ornamentation

Many books have been written on the subject of ornamentation, which is a very complex one, since there are different rules for almost every composer. Dollé, for example, found it necessary to preface his pieces with the suggestion that: 'if anyone finds himself in difficulty over some passage he need only do me the honour of calling at my house. It would give me great pleasure to show him my way of playing the ornaments.' The following notes, therefore, provide only a brief introduction concentrating on the practical aspects that are most relevant to viol players.

Ornaments in French music are extremely important and should not be changed or added to. Try to play them all as marked and do not use any vibrato unless it is specifically indicated. Practise the more complex pieces without ornaments but with the required fingering (which may well be different from that for an unornamented version) to make sure that the basic tune still comes through. Play the ornaments as freely as possible without losing the main pulse, using very little bow on the actual ornament, as otherwise it will assume too much importance. Fig. 26 shows the ornaments, signs, and terms found in the music of Marais, which are fairly typical of those used by French composers of the period, although, as mentioned above, each writer has his own idiosyncrasies.

Trills normally start on the note above the written one, and often have a long appoggiatura, so that the upper note is held for half or more of the written note. The appoggiatura provides the tension and the trill the relaxation, so try to relax the left hand when trilling and lighten pressure on the bow.

Most trills of any length sound better if they speed up gradually, and the overall speed should be in keeping with the type of movement—trills in slow movements should start more slowly.

Use a slow bow on all trills, fast or slow, and try to rest for a short time on the written note before going on to the next, otherwise the main (written) note will be lost. However, take care not to accent the written note when you stop trilling.

On very long trills there is often a problem for the bow as the rhythm is ♩ ♩. ♪ . In such cases the bow can be lifted off after the long note and put back very near the tip to play the last quaver.

Mordents are almost always inverted (played downwards) and should normally be fast, with the first (written) note on the beat. Be careful not to accent the last note of the three or it will sound as if the first two are before the beat. Play the mordent the same way as you would if it were just one note, so that, for

3.7. French Suites 125

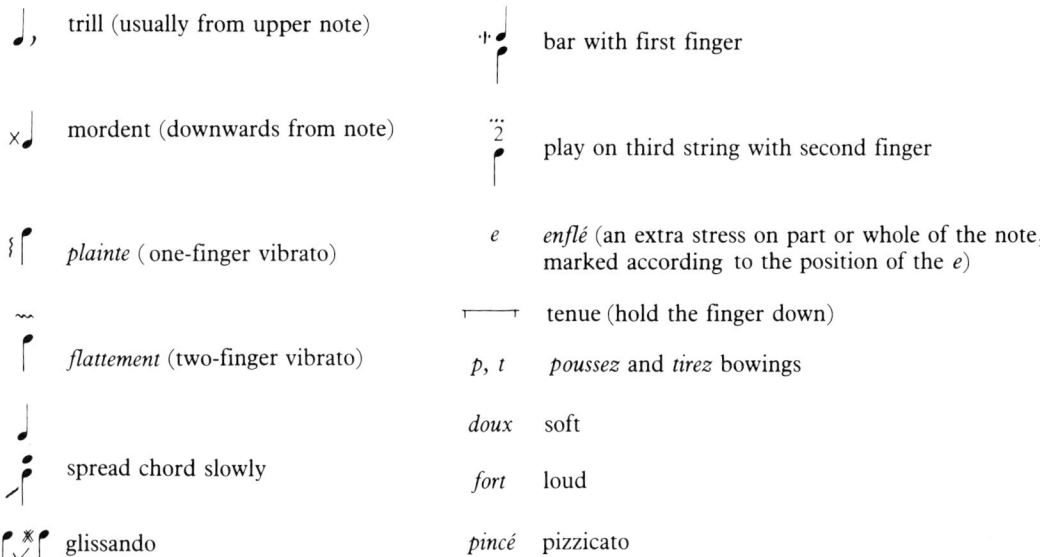

Fig. 26. Ornaments, signs, and terms found in Marais

example, the last beat of a bar in triple time is as light as usual, even when ornamented.

Vibrato can be used as an ornament in most of the solo repertoire; it should not be used constantly but only to intensify the sound of particular notes. There are two types of vibrato in French music, the *plainte* and the *flattement*. For the *plainte*, a normal vibrato with one finger (usually the fourth), put the finger on the fret (not behind it) and roll the finger slowly to either side of the fret, rotating the hand from the wrist. It is usually easier to lift the other fingers off, and if necessary bunch them up behind the vibrating finger to give more strength. The *plainte* should develop from nothing to a slow movement with a wide amplitude. Then gradually speed up the vibrations while decreasing the amplitude.

The *flattement* is done by placing two fingers very close to each other with the lower finger behind the fret and using the normal vibrato movement, allowing the upper finger to touch the string gently just above the fret but not pressing it down fully. This should give a very small pitch variation, not so much that it sounds like a trill. On the lower strings it is sometimes more effective to beat the upper finger, as one would in a trill, still keeping it very close to the lower finger.

The *enflé* (*e*) requires a combination of bow speed and pressure. Where the *e* comes at the beginning of a note, use a faster bow to project the sound. Where it comes later in the note, increase the intensity by using more pressure. *Enflés* are only written where extra stress is needed.

## 3.7. French Suites

### Examples from Marais

Ex. 66 gives one of Marais's simpler movements, the Menuet from the Suite in A minor. Play it first without any ornaments, but including the slurs. Then gradually introduce the ornaments, keeping them light. Notice that the bowing nearly always follows the pattern ♩ ♩. As usual with this type of rhythm, the problem is to get back to the point without accenting every crotchet.

The notes in small print are to be played fast, like ornaments, and as late as possible. Small print is used whenever the time taken to play the notes concerned is not allowed for in the bar, as in bar 13 of Ex. 66, where the main note is written as a dotted minim even though four semiquavers are to follow. The *enflé* in bar 2 indicates that the first bar should be felt as an unstressed 'up bar' to the second.

In Ex. 67, from the Prelude in G major, the fingering (Marais's own) is all across the strings, to allow pairs of notes to sound together. The hand will need to be dropped as described in Section 2.3 to help with the string crossing, but at this speed little arm movement should be necessary. Give a good stress on each change of harmony.

Fig. 27, a facsimile extract from Marais's *Troisième livre*, includes one of his longest slurs, consisting of thirty-six notes. The faster you play the easier it becomes. Marais is meticulous about always having the bow the right way round, and in this case the long slur comes on a back bow. The chord before the end is quite hard to find in the panic after such a slur. Practise putting down the chord from the previous two notes, and remember also to put down a finger for the appoggiatura at the same time. Notice that the slur on to the last bar means that the final chord can be on the forward bow. Marais thinks of everything!

Ex. 66. Marais, Menuet from Suite in A minor (*Cinquième livre*)

3.7. French Suites 127

Ex. 67. Marais, Prelude in G major (*Deuxième livre*)

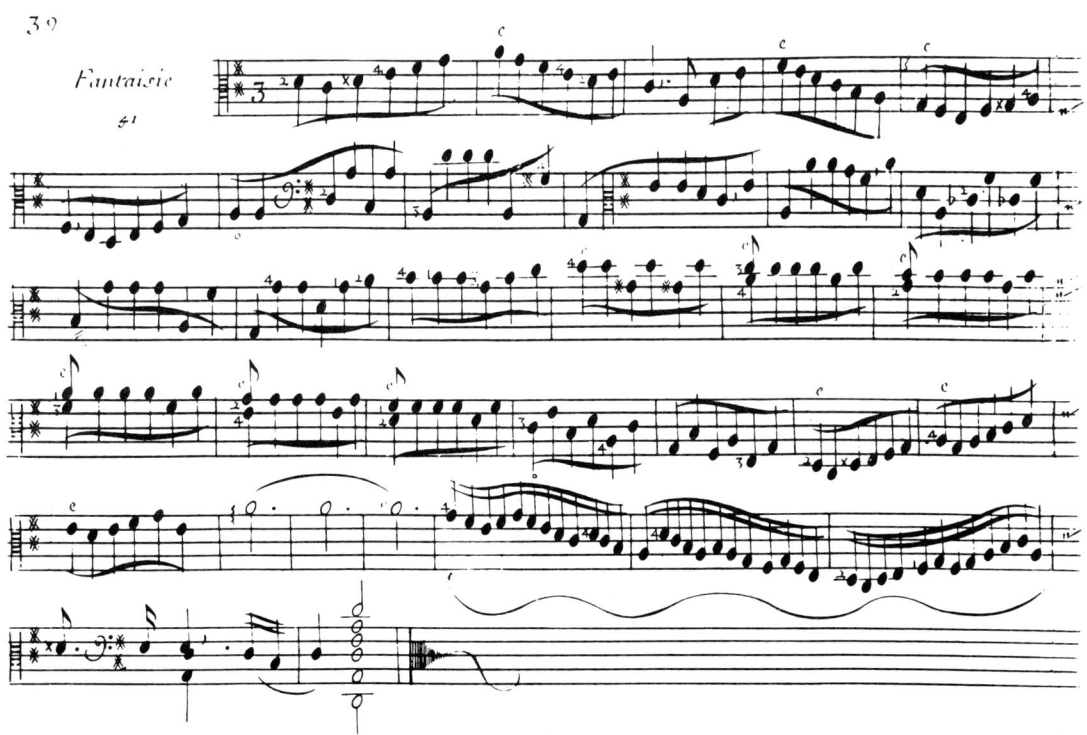

Fig. 27. Marais, *Fantasie* from *Troisième livre* (facsimile)

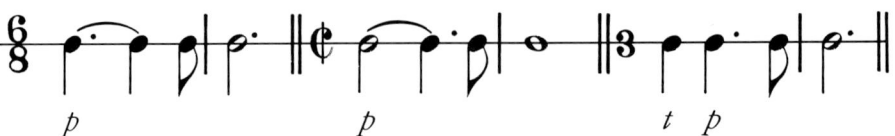

Ex. 68. Dotted rhythms in Marais

Ex. 69. Marais, *Sonnerie de Ste Geneviève*

Ex. 68 shows some of the many different dotted rhythms that occur constantly in Marais. The problem as ever is to avoid 'banging' the short note, and it is worth practising the rhythm on one note as shown to eliminate this fault. Use the bowings indicated, always decreasing pressure on the *tirez* stroke, and sometimes taking the bow off the string after the long note, as described earlier.

Marais sometimes uses special effects in his pieces. An example occurs in *Sonnerie de Ste Geneviève* (Ex. 69) for violin, viol, and continuo, where he writes bowings on repeated notes. This means playing four separate notes in each bow, very fast, which is quite difficult to achieve. Try to make the bow bounce along the string like a stone skimming on water.

Marais sometimes marks *pincé*, meaning pizzicato, often alternating rather quickly with bowed phrases. A better sound can sometimes be obtained by plucking with the thumb rather than the fingers. At the end of the *Cinquième livre*, 'Le Tast' makes use of left-hand percussion. The notes are sounded by hammering the fingers down on the string without plucking with the right hand. This is extremely difficult and you may be pleased to see that an easier, bowed alternative is given for the whole piece.

Marais often uses descriptive titles, some of which clearly indicate character pieces. One of the most famous is his *Tableau de l'opération de la taille*, a dramatic musical account with spoken narration of the operation for a bladder stone which Marais himself underwent, without benefit of modern anaesthetics.

# 4
# Practising, Ensemble Playing, and Performing

## 4.1. How to Practise

The amount of time you are able to give to viol practice is a matter of individual choice and circumstance, but even with very short practice periods it is possible to improve steadily. Regularity is more important than length; twenty minutes a day is better than a three-hour session once a week. The less time you have, the more efficiently you must use it. The basic principle is to decide what aspects of technique or which particular bars or phrases are causing the most difficulty and practise those more intensively on their own. Playing through whole pieces is the slowest way to improve them; repetition of small sections is the most effective.

Some people enjoy practising by using a book of exercises, of which there are several available (see Appendix 3). However it can be just as good, if not better, to use specific technical difficulties in the pieces you are playing as a basis for more detailed study; then you are practising the difficult passages you will actually have to master, rather than hypothetical examples of problems you might come across.

### Bowing

You should always spend a little time, even most of it in the early stages, making a beautiful sound playing something very easy, perhaps just one note or a simple scale. Experiment with different combinations of bow speed, pressure, and distance from the bridge to get the best possible sound. Practise the two bow strokes and bow changes, and shape the notes by using different types of attack and ending, as described in Section 1.4.

To focus attention on the bowing aspect of a piece you are working on, play the rhythm of a few bars on one note. As you play, imagine the tune and concentrate on deciding how much bow speed and pressure you need for each note, which part of the bow you need to be in, and how you want each note to begin and end. When you can make the bow do what you want on one note, play with the left hand as well.

String crossing is another aspect of bowing which frequently causes problems. Practise different patterns such as those suggested in Sections 1.4 and 2.3, repeating them many times until the bowing arm automatically moves the right distance with the minimum of effort. Make sure that every note after a string crossing begins clearly by gripping the string with the bow before you play.

## Fingering

Like bowing, fingering should sometimes be practised alone. This may be done by playing pizzicato or with the left hand only. Plucking can show you how well you have placed your fingers by the amount of resonance produced. If the fingers are not up to the fret, the strings will buzz against the fret or go dead immediately. Playing with the left hand only will show up any weakness in the fingers. All the notes should be clearly audible except when starting from open strings, but if the finger movement is too slow there will be no sound.

Practise the fingering exercises in Parts 1, 2, and 3, and make quite sure that you are holding your fingers down, especially when crossing strings. Play the exercises at a variety of speeds and look at your fingers sometimes to check that they are only making the minimum necessary movement.

Practise finding simple chords and double stops, looking at your fingers if necessary, until they learn to go down in pairs or larger groups. Build up bigger chords gradually, first playing the bass note alone, then gradually adding more notes until you can put the whole chord shape down, just as a keyboard player would. For more detailed advice on practising chords, see Section 2.4.

When practising difficult shifts, play the notes before and after the position change many times, using the correct fingers, until judging exactly how far to move becomes automatic, like a reflex. Also practise using the left hand only, as described above. The shifting movement must be very fast to avoid gaps in the sound.

## Co-ordination

Co-ordination takes time to develop and needs a great deal of practice to become reliable at faster speeds. The fingers tend to move more slowly than the bow, especially when lifting off. Extend the exercises in Section 2.3 and practise bowed-out trills such as those found at the end of Simpson's divisions. Playford gives some good advice: 'In the practice of any lesson play it slow at first and by often practice it will bring your hand to a more swift motion.'

A metronome is a great help in building up speed gradually. Start at a tempo you can easily manage and raise the metronome setting one mark at a time until bow and fingers start to disagree. Make a note of the setting and go back to a slower speed. Then each time you practise start at a slightly higher metronome setting and try to increase the maximum speed at which you can achieve good co-ordination.

## Learning new pieces

In approaching a new piece you need to strike a balance between working on the technical aspects and thinking of the shape and character of the music. First, play through to get an overall idea of the piece, sketching in the difficult bits, or even missing them out. Next work from the beginning, marking the passages that present the biggest problems. Try out alternative fingerings and bowings until you are sure which you prefer, or which sounds better. If beauty of sound is your criterion, the easiest fingering may not be the best.

In some cases the bowing and fingering will be influenced by the phrasing; for example, you should normally arrange for the most important note of a phrase to fall on a forward bow and avoid shifting where two notes need to be very legato.

There may still be some bars that are too difficult to play at this stage, but try to imagine how you would like them to sound and aim towards that. Practise them extremely slowly to begin with, but take care to keep the chosen tempo strict. Repeat them many times slowly, but occasionally try them up to speed to see how close you are getting to your objective. Do not allow any bad sound to go past without analysing why it is unsatisfactory (see Sections 1.5 and 2.1). This is important whether you are playing slowly or fast.

As suggested earlier, you should sometimes make a point of playing through, if not the entire piece, at least an extended section of it, concentrating on the music rather than the technical problems. Look for points of tension and relaxation in the harmonic sequence and decide where the high and low points of the melody are. Mark in ends of phrases, dynamics, and articulation. Study the accompaniment if there is one, as this will give you a better overall view of the piece.

When you play, exaggerate everything you decided: for example, make big breathing spaces between phrases, crescendo to fortissimo and diminuendo to pianissimo; aim for a very smooth legato and a very short staccato, and also practise at speeds more extreme than you finally intend. Most people are far too subtle in their musical ideas, with the result that everything comes out sounding rather boring. It is much easier to tone down an over-enthusiastic interpretation than to enliven a dull one.

However much or little time you have to practise, the most important thing is concentration. Occasionally you may find yourself going through the motions of playing the notes while thinking about something completely different. It is very easy if you are a busy person to do this kind of 'practice' but quite useless. Better to spend less time and be able to keep your mind firmly on the specific objective.

Decide how long you have on each occasion and plan what in particular you want to practise in that time. It might be just five minutes bowing open strings and aiming for the most beautiful sound you can achieve, or it could be ten minutes on two difficult bars of a piece you are learning. Preferably this would be part of a longer practice period, but even a very short time well used can be valuable.

## Sight-reading

It is very important to be able to sight-read unfamiliar music without stopping every few bars, whether you are playing with other people or simply looking for a new piece to learn. For this reason you should regularly include sight-reading in your practice schedule. Before you begin, take note of the key and time signatures and think of a speed that looks feasible for most of the piece, even though it may be too fast for a few of the hardest passages. If you take too slow a tempo it can make nonsense of the music.

Even if you find it hard to imagine how a piece will sound by looking at it, try to pick out patterns, such as parts of scales and arpeggios, octave leaps, or repeated phrases. In fast passages, look for the first and last notes, and try to play those on the right beat, filling in the ones between as best you can. It is always better to miss out difficult notes than to slow down. Cutting long notes too short is another common fault, and there is also a great temptation to rush over easy bars, especially when they are followed by something harder. Try playing with a metronome sometimes to help keep the time steady.

When sight reading you are unlikely to have time to consider the finer points of bowing and fingering, except at the beginning of a phrase. The important things to aim for are the rhythm and notes, in that order. As your reading improves you will find that you also understand the phrasing more quickly and can correct the bowing as you go along.

## Playing from memory

Some people who find sight-reading very difficult have the compensation of being able to memorize quite easily. The converse is also true, and players who can read through almost anything are sometimes unable to play the simplest tune without music.

In earlier times much music was never written down but passed from one musician to another. This is the ideal way of learning from memory, because you never have to make the transition from playing with the music to playing without. However, since the tradition of learning by rote has been largely lost in the twentieth century, most people will have to learn first from the music and then try to do without it.

Begin with a short piece, and learn it phrase by phrase, singing each one before you try to play it. Gradually build up the piece in your mind until you can remember the whole thing. You may find that your performance of the piece once you have memorized it is more musically satisfying. This is one of the great benefits of learning to play from memory: it focuses the attention on the structure of the music. In time you will begin to take in whole phrases instead of individual notes, and thorough practice on simple pieces will enable you to tackle progressively more complex ones. You might find it a useful transitional device to make a recording, playing from the music, and then play along with the tape.

Group playing from memory is even rarer in our time, though the tradition has been revived by a few professional ensembles, with very good results. Choose a simple dance to start with, and have some people playing from music at first so that the players without music are not put off by too many other parts faltering. When you can all play your parts without music you will be amazed at the very different feeling that results: you will have a much stronger sense of playing together rather than of concentrating on the music in front of you with an occasional ear for the other parts.

## Getting help

Individual lessons with an encouraging teacher can greatly speed up the process of learning and make playing and practising more enjoyable by giving you something to aim for. A teacher who is familiar with the viol repertoire can also introduce you to new music and suggest pieces which are right for your current state of technical development.

Ideally you should have some lessons right at the beginning, because it is much harder to unlearn bad habits than to learn correctly in the first place. At later stages people are sometimes reluctant to have lessons, either because they think the teacher may condemn them to going back to basics or because they feel they have no piece sufficiently polished to justify a lesson. However, it may be that small technical faults are preventing you from making progress and even one lesson can give you enough ideas to carry on alone for several months.

If you live too far from any viol teacher to have regular lessons, you may be able to get a certain amount of help from other viol players, or from good musicians who are familiar with Renaissance and Baroque style and can comment on the musical aspects of your playing.

## Concerts and recordings

Listening to viol music well played in concerts and recordings can also be very helpful in giving you an idea of what to aim for in terms of sound and style, as well as expanding your knowledge of the repertoire. You may not often get the opportunity to hear a solo viol recital or a consort of viols, but in the absence of live concerts there is much to be learnt from repeated hearings of the many good recordings now available.

Although these by no means cover the repertoire, most periods and styles of viol playing are represented, and a recommended list is given in the Discography. If possible buy or borrow a recording of pieces which you are studying. Do not become discouraged because it sounds so different from your own performance. This is not entirely due to your inferior skill; recordings are often heavily edited and the sound adjusted to enhance the richness of tone and the prominence of the soloist, besides eliminating the small slips which even the best performers are liable to make in the concert hall.

You can also learn by listening to a wide variety of music of the period to develop your knowledge of its character and style, a most important aspect of viol playing.

# 4.2. Playing in Ensembles and Consorts

Try to find opportunities for playing with other people as well as practising on your own. Apart from the pleasure to be had from playing the viol in congenial company, it will give you a chance to read through new music and increase your ability to make the best use of whatever technique you have.

## 4.2. Playing in Ensembles and Consorts

Playing in a consort should be like having an interesting discussion with a group of friends, where each person makes his point clear but also listens to the others. Too often a viol consort can sound like an angry argument where everyone talks but no one listens.

As the following quotation from Mace (1676) illustrates, this is not a new problem:

> We would never allow any performer to overtop or outcry another by Loud Play, but our great care was, to have all the Parts equally heard, by which means (though sometimes we had but indifferent or mean Hands to perform with) yet this caution made the Musick lovely, and very contentive.

Although it is essential in consort playing to recognize which are the important points in your own part, and make sure that they are clearly heard, often these points will only be a few bars or even two or three notes, after which you should retreat again to allow other parts to come through.

The most distinctive feature of sixteenth- and seventeenth-century consort music is its polyphonic character. Unlike classical string quartets, where the lower parts are often accompanying the first violin, all the parts of a viol fantasia are independent, and, as Mace says, of equal importance. This leads to particular difficulties, one of which is the problem of keeping your place. The rhythm often bears little relation to the bar lines, which in any case are usually a later addition, and it is very hard to feel where the strong beats should be. The parts seldom start together and many phrases overlap, making the cadences much harder to find. The exception to this is dance music, but even here the cross-rhythms can be so strong that it is easy to lose the beat.

Another problem at first is the notation generally used in viol music, with the minim as the basic beat instead of the crotchet normally found in later music. Although most people soon learn to count in minims, it is harder to remember that a minim rest represents one beat instead of two, and it is also more difficult to distinguish, especially at speed, between minim ▬ and semibreve ▬ rests than between crotchet and minim rests. If a consort piece continually goes wrong in the same place, the most likely explanation is that one of the players is miscounting a rest.

Keeping a steady pulse is essential. Often a piece will fall apart because one member of the ensemble is hesitating fractionally to search for the more difficult notes, thus shaking the rhythm.

The enjoyment of consort playing can be completely spoiled by bad feeling amongst the players, however technically proficient they may be. A few suggestions may help to avoid difficulties.

## 4.2. Playing in Ensembles and Consorts

Unless one member of the consort is very much more experienced than the others, the 'leader' is normally the player of the highest part that is playing at any particular time, or sometimes, when this is a slow-moving part, the player with the fastest moving part. Whoever is leading should indicate the tempo with a clear nod, making sure that everyone is ready to play before giving an up-beat to begin. It should not be necessary to count aloud, except occasionally on a first run-through to establish the tempo, or when one of the players is in difficulty. However, if you notice that someone is lost and you are sure that you are in the right place, count a few beats and then give a bar number to help them to get back in. If you get lost yourself, and are unable to find your place, drop out and ask for a bar number. It is pointless to press on when several players are out. Better to stop and restart at an appropriate place, such as the beginning of a new section (not always the beginning of the piece).

Be considerate about tuning. It is almost impossible to tune properly while other people are playing or even talking. If you have a problem in your part, try to solve it silently, or at least wait until no one is tuning. It is a waste of time to tune simultaneously with another player unless you are tuning to each other. Patience while other people tune is absolutely essential.

When you make a mistake, there is no need to apologize or give explanations. If you find yourself repeatedly losing your place, suggest playing something easier rather than struggling on unsuccessfully. You cannot possibly enjoy playing if you are in a constant state of anxiety, and the more experienced players may get impatient, though they should remember that they were probably in the same position not so long ago.

A satisfying consort session depends on choosing suitable pieces and playing them at a speed within the competence of the least advanced member of the group. If that is unacceptably slow from a musical point of view, the piece is too difficult, and it would be better to take parts home to practise for the next meeting. However, it is sometimes possible to play pieces at an appropriate speed by missing out or simplifying the more difficult notes. The ability to keep in time with the other players regardless of technical difficulties is a very important skill to acquire in all types of ensemble playing.

If you play consort music on a regular basis you will find that many of the problems mentioned disappear. You can then concentrate on finer points of interpretation, phrasing, and tone colour. To improve further it is a good idea to invite someone to coach you, preferably on a piece that you know well enough to play without difficulty. A piece which has reached the stage of being accurate but not very interesting can be brought to musical life by an experienced consort coach in the course of an hour, a most rewarding experience for the players.

Another good way to improve your playing is to attend workshops and summer schools. These vary in length from one day to three weeks, some specializing in ensemble playing and others concentrating on solo repertoire. They provide an excellent opportunity for meeting other players, and a few days of intensive coaching and playing can lift your standard quite noticeably. They are normally advertised in early music journals and newsletters.

## 4.3. Performing

At some point in your viol-playing career it is quite likely that you will find yourself performing in public. This may be in a domestic situation for a few friends or a full-scale concert in a large hall. Whatever the event, playing to other people requires a different approach from playing for yourself. Rehearsing for a public performance can provide a very useful focus for practice, both individual and in groups. Taking part in a successful performance is most satisfying, and you may sometimes have the pleasure of introducing the viol to people who have not encountered it before.

However, even if you are not consciously nervous, an audience can have a surprising effect on your playing. Although some people are inspired by the occasion, it is much more common to play less well than usual. You may find your bow shaking uncontrollably on long notes or make mistakes where you never have before. Anxiety also affects the ability to keep a steady pulse, which makes polyphonic music especially hazardous for inexperienced performers.

You can minimize the risk of mishaps by observing a few general guidelines. Choose pieces which are not technically difficult for you and learn them very thoroughly. This means continuing to practise a piece with full concentration even when you feel you can already play it perfectly. Then, if something does go wrong, you are much more likely to find your place again, probably without anyone noticing.

If you do make a mistake, try not to let it appear on your face, put it out of your mind, and think only of what is still to come. In ensembles it is sensible to have a contingency plan. Carefully note points where all the parts come together so that players will know where to come in again if necessary, or agree that one player will give a definite nod or a bar number if the ensemble becomes unsteady.

If you get involved in planning a concert programme, make sure that it is not too long. Most early music concerts are composed of many short pieces, which makes it vital to allow for the time between as well as the actual music. This has to include tuning, any spoken material, applause, and possibly changes of instrument. Try to avoid the necessity for a player to pick up a different instrument for just one piece, and group short pieces together, making this clear on the programme, so that the applause is limited in frequency.

Variety is not normally a problem with groups of mixed instruments, especially if singers are included, but a programme with just viols needs careful planning to avoid monotony. Fantasies in particular tend to sound very similar to listeners, so restrict their number and maintain interest by including other forms such as dance movements. It is also helpful to vary the number of players.

When you play for an audience, it is essential to emphasize strongly all aspects of your playing: dynamics, phrasing, and articulation. You know what you are trying to do, but your audience does not, and it is most unlikely that the effect will sound exaggerated to them. Try to face the audience as much as possible and make them feel that you are communicating with them as well as enjoying yourself. Keeping music stands low helps to reduce the barrier between players and listeners.

When playing the viol in an orchestra, especially with 'modern' instruments, you are very likely to find yourself drowned, either because there are too many other players or the hall is too big. You will have to project the sound as much as possible by using plenty of bow and playing nearer the bridge than usual. In a resonant acoustic you will have to play notes shorter, using very clear articulation.

Another problem is tuning, often more difficult in concerts. It is a good idea to leave the instruments out on stage for as long as possible beforehand to adjust to the temperature and humidity of the concert venue. Tune very carefully before the audience come in and aim to tune as little as possible during the concert. Fiddling with pegs between pieces is often a sign of nerves, and players may end up altering a string that was perfectly well in tune. A stable tuning source is essential—the harpsichord if you are using one, otherwise an electronic tuning meter, or the most stable instrument.

Too much movement on the platform can distract from the music. Many famous performers are guilty of moving around a lot when they play, but most of the viol treatises refer to the importance of not moving more than necessary. Ganassi (1542–3) clearly felt strongly about it: 'If you were to move the whole upper part of your body to and fro when you move your hand it would be as unpleasant a sight as if a master were to take the broom from his servant's hands and sweep the floor himself.'

# 5
# Viols and Bows

## 5.1. Buying a Viol

Points to consider when you decide to buy a viol include the size, type of model, whether to buy new or secondhand, and of course the price.

The question of size is very much a personal thing, but you need to think about whether you are more likely to play mainly in consort, mainly solo music, or a mixture of the two. If you plan to play regularly with others, your choice may be influenced by what sizes of instrument they already have and what kind of music you play with them. Physical factors are also relevant, such as which size of instrument feels most comfortable for you to hold and whether you have problems stretching on a larger instrument.

Bass is certainly the most versatile size and probably the most useful, especially if you are the only viol player in your area. It also has a large solo repertoire. Tenor is the easiest size for beginners and a very useful instrument for consort music, but has virtually no solo repertoire of its own. The treble is always more exposed being on top, and it depends on your personality whether you see this as an advantage or not. It is perhaps more difficult to achieve a good sound on treble in the early stages. A further drawback is the relatively small amount of solo music.

The actual size of instruments varies greatly within each tuning; for example, a large tenor could be the same size as a small bass. Whatever size you choose initially, you will not find it difficult to change or to add to your collection of viols later, as they are all played in basically the same way. There are also some less common sizes of viol, the normal tunings of which are shown in Fig. 28.

Having decided on the size, the next question is which type of model to select. Early Renaissance viols, which often have no soundpost, are only suitable if your interest lies mainly in sixteenth-century music (Fig. 29). Even then you should find out if other players you know have the same type, as these viols sound quite different from the later ones and do not blend well with them, though they do sound good with Renaissance wind instruments.

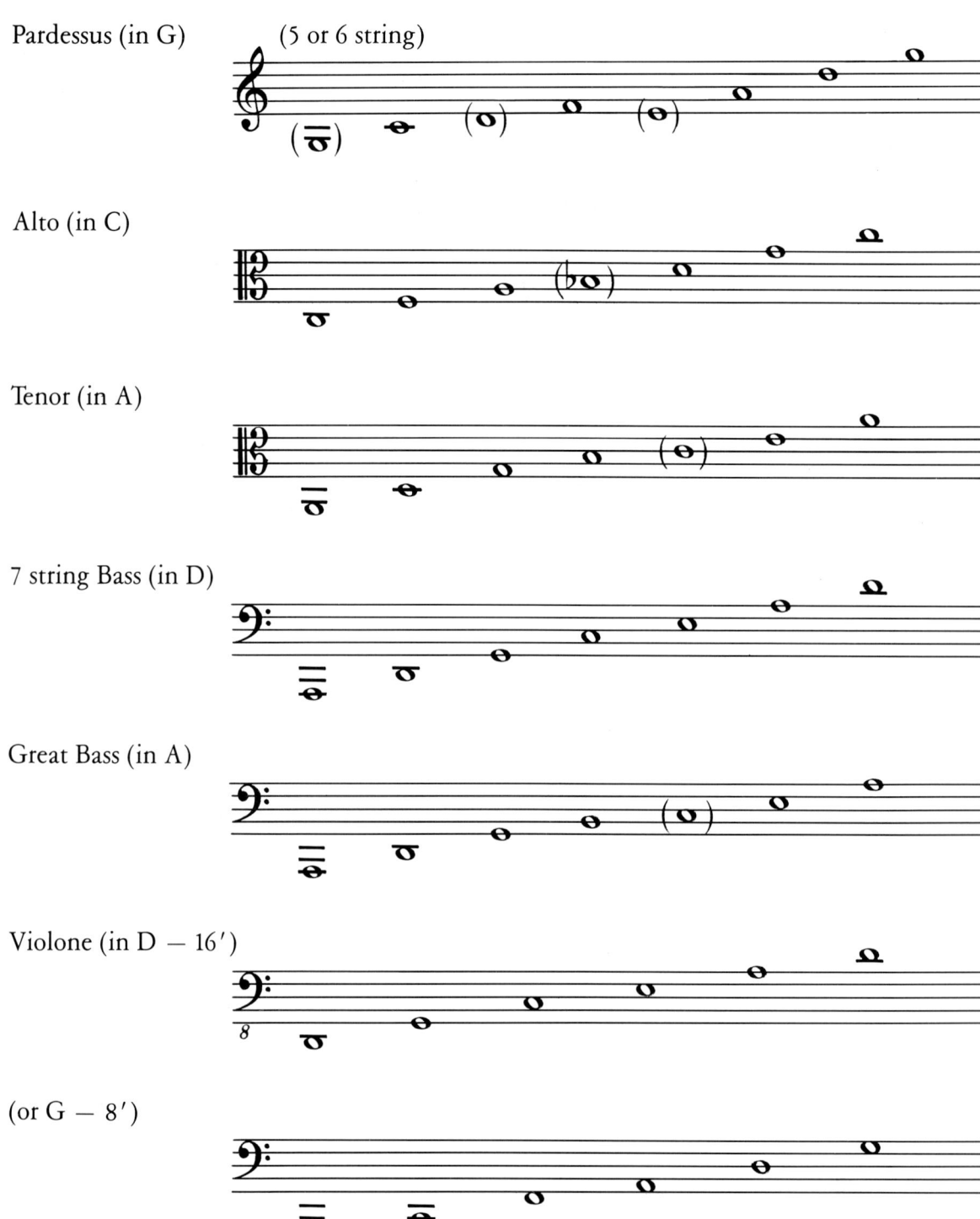

Fig. 28. Less common viols and their tunings

5.1. *Buying a Viol* 141

If, on the other hand, your main interest is in Baroque music, you might consider a seven-string bass (Fig. 30). Although almost all the solo music of this period is playable with six strings, the French repertoire often includes the bottom A and it can also be useful for continuo playing. The disadvantages are that such viols can be rather overpowering in consort music, they speak more slowly, and in the early stages it is harder to find the right string.

As an all-purpose instrument the English type of viol is probably the most practical (Figs. 31–4), either a consort instrument copied from the early

Fig. 29. Renaissance viol after Ciciliano (*c.*1560) by Martin Edmunds

Fig. 30. Seven-string bass viol after Bertrand (1704) by Robert Eyland

## 5.1. Buying a Viol

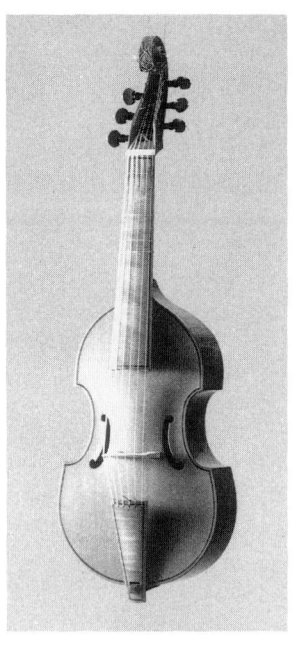 

Fig. 31. *(far left)* Treble viol after Jaye (*c.*1630) by Neil Hansford

Fig. 32. *(left)* Alto viol after Jaye (1662) by Norman Myall

seventeenth-century makers such as Jaye or Rose, or, if you will be playing more later music, one modelled after Barak Norman or Meares.

The simplest way to choose a viol is to visit an early music shop and try out whatever is in stock, not necessarily to buy but at least to get some ideas. Summer schools and courses where many players with their different instruments come together also provide good opportunities for trying out various models, and you may also find viols offered for sale. Buying a viol secondhand can often be an advantage, since most string instruments improve with age and any problems of adjustment should have been remedied. A new viol changes considerably in the first year or so, usually for the better, but any faults in construction or materials may also appear during this time.

A new viol will need playing in before it begins to produce its best sound. To do this play strongly on every string and every fret as often and as long as possible. This will help the natural resonances of the instrument to develop to the full and it will gradually speak more easily. All viols improve with playing and even an old viol may feel stiff if it is not played for several weeks.

Many people buy their first viol 'ready made' but later decide to commission

5.1. *Buying a Viol*  143

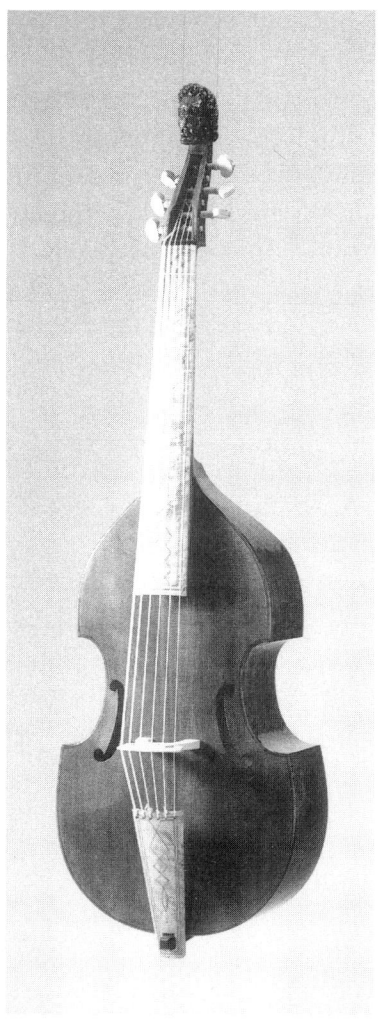 

Fig. 33. Tenor viol after Rose (1598) by David Rubio

Fig. 34. Bass viol after Rose (1595) by Robert Eyland

one from a maker. This allows you to choose the exact model you want and also to specify woods, finishes, and any particular decoration. You may also have an instrument specially adapted to your needs, for example a bass with a short string length if you have small hands. The disadvantage is that you may have to wait several months or years to get it, and you cannot be absolutely sure how it will feel and sound.

Prices vary enormously and do not always correspond with quality. The best makers are usually expensive but less good ones are not always cheap.

Occasionally you may find a good secondhand viol being sold cheaply and young makers often begin by charging low prices even though their instruments can be excellent. Consult an experienced player if you can, and try out several viols before making a choice. It is a mistake to think that beginners should make do with cheap viols. A good instrument will help your playing from the start, and will also be much easier to sell should you decide to make a change.

## 5.2. Viol Maintenance and Adjustment

Changes in humidity can put a strain on viols, as on any wooden instrument. The main problem is not so much the natural climate, though extremes will affect the strings and make the tuning unstable, but central heating, which can open up joints, cause cracks and interfere with the adjustment of the soundpost (see below). You may need to use an artificial humidifier which is available from string dealers and hangs inside the instrument.

The varnish on a viol can be spoiled by an excessive buildup of dust, sweat, or rosin. This can be avoided by dusting regularly. You may occasionally polish it with a varnish reviver or with antique furniture polish, but, if you have a new viol, avoid doing this during the first six months as the varnish can take that long to harden. Be careful not to leave the viol in the sun or you may find it stuck to its case.

When you buy a viol it should be set up to sound its best by the maker or dealer, but you cannot rely on this. In addition, the viol may alter over a period of time. Various parts of the instrument might need adjusting, including the bridge, nut, soundpost, pegs, strings and frets. For some problems you will have to seek professional help, but others are more easily remedied.

### Bridge, nut, and soundpost

The bridge should be evenly curved so that you can play all the strings equally easily without touching adjacent ones. If, having mastered basic bowing technique, you are still frequently hitting two strings at once, your bridge curve may need altering. A temporary measure is to put a tiny piece of leather or paper under a string that is too low or to enlarge the groove in the bridge with a needle file if the string is too high. The latter is a delicate operation as the bridge will be ruined if you go too far.

The strings should be close to the fingerboard all the way up so that they can be pressed down easily, but not so close that the strings buzz against the frets when plucked. The height of the string from the fingerboard is determined by the nut and the bridge height, which should be adjusted to give a comfortable action. This is a highly skilled job and needs to be done by a viol maker or repairer.

The feet of the bridge should be perfectly fitted to the belly of the instrument. The tailpiece side should be at right angles to the belly, and the front side slightly sloping. A common defect is the tilting of the bridge towards the peg box as a result of constant tuning. This needs checking regularly because, if it is not corrected, the tone will suffer and eventually the bridge may warp and need replacing.

To straighten the bridge, hold the viol firmly between the knees, grasp the top of the bridge with both hands between thumb and fingers, and gradually shift it back to a vertical position.

The sound of a viol is greatly affected by the position of the soundpost and can often be much improved by slight adjustment. This again is a job for the original maker or a string-instrument repairer.

## Pegs

Few things about a viol are more crucial than the fit of the pegs. They should turn smoothly and then stay where they are put. Peg paste, available from violin dealers, often helps. Otherwise sticking pegs can sometimes be eased by being rubbed with soap and slipping ones may be treated with chalk. If several pegs need treatment, deal with them one at a time; avoid letting down several strings at once, or you run the risk of causing the bridge or even the soundpost to fall down.

If this treatment fails to improve the pegs, it may be that the holes in the peg box are not perfectly round, or that the peg is incorrectly tapered so that it only fits on one side of the peg box. A repairer should be able to remedy this, though sometimes new pegs may be required.

If the pegs turn well but the string still moves in jumps when tuning, it may be sticking at the nut or bridge. To avoid this, rub the grooves at these two points with a soft pencil and check that they are wide enough not to grip the string. When strings break, note exactly where this happened; if at the nut or tailpiece, it is probably due to a sharp edge, which should be filed down.

## Strings

Your choice of stringing can make a big difference to the sound and feel of a viol, indeed can almost change it into a different instrument. Fig. 35 shows some of the

## 5.2. Viol Maintenance and Adjustment

Fig. 35. Types of string. (*from top to bottom*) plain gut (thin); plain gut (thick); catline (thin); catline (thick); open wound on plain gut; open wound on catline; overspun on plain gut; overspun on catline

different types of string available. Overspun strings (gut wound with various metals) were probably not used until the middle of the seventeenth century, so if you are planning to play mostly Renaissance music you should consider all-gut stringing. One advantage of using gut strings for consort music is that, having a shorter resonance and more focused sound, they allow individual lines to be heard more clearly. They also stay better in tune.

Plain gut gives a good sound on the top strings, but the thicker ones are less satisfactory unless they have extra twist. For the lower strings you will need catlines, made of strands of gut twisted together like a rope. This gives much more elasticity and therefore a better sound than very thick plain gut.

For later music the bottom two or three strings should be overspun to get the full resonance from the instrument. A gut fourth string open wound with metal can provide a good transition between gut and overspun strings. If you want to play the whole range of viol music with as authentic a sound as possible, you might consider changing the bottom two strings as appropriate. It would be tiresome to do this often and a better long-term solution is probably to have different viols for different types of music.

There are other decisions to be made about strings. A heavily built viol needs heavier (thicker) strings, whereas a very light instrument will usually respond better with thinner ones. On the other hand, strings that are too light produce a thin, reedy sound that lacks body. Certainly for solo playing, heavier strings may be needed to make the sound project.

Another factor to consider is the string length (measured from bridge to nut) of the instrument in question. For example, a bass viol with a comparatively long string length for its pitch will need slightly thinner strings than a shorter instrument of the same pitch, otherwise the tension will be too great. Keep a record of your string measurements and experiment with thinner or thicker ones when you replace strings until you are confident that you have the best stringing for your instrument.

Good-quality strings should be true; that is, the interval between the open string and any given fret will be the same on all strings. Unfortunately, as strings get older, they go false. This means that they will play too sharp on all the frets, the error increasing with the number of frets. This explains why a note at the fifth fret is not always the same as the next open string, even when the fourth between the strings sounds in tune. Small adjustments can be made by moving frets to improve the tuning, but eventually the only remedy is to change the string.

Most of the instruments on which modern copies are based were probably played at a lower pitch than the standard $a' = 440$. This is why viols often sound better tuned a semitone below modern pitch ($a' = 415$), or even a whole tone lower ($a' = 390$). The lower pitch gives less tension on the strings and a pleasant, more gentle sound. Top strings may also last longer. Early Renaissance viols, on the other hand, seem to work better at modern pitch or a semitone higher.

If you have to change pitch, for example to play with wind instruments, try to do this several hours in advance if possible, to give the strings time to settle, otherwise they will tend to creep back to the previous pitch.

## Changing strings

Strings will need replacing when they break, become hairy or frayed, or go false as described above. Save old strings, as they can be used in emergencies if unbroken and the gut can be reused for tying frets. When handling a new string, be careful not to kink it as this will make a weak point, causing it to break more quickly.

To attach a new string, start with the tailpiece end first. For overspun strings, which have a prepared loop at one end, thread the other end of the string through the hole in the tailpiece, then pass it through the loop and pull tight. For thin gut strings you will need to make your own loop, as shown in Fig. 36. This is not possible with thick gut, which should either be knotted or have the end burnt to

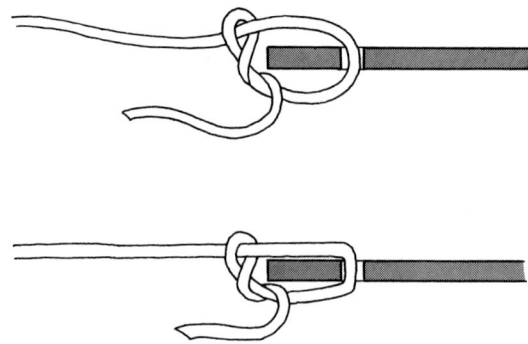

Fig. 36. Attaching the string at the tailpiece

prevent the string from pulling through the hole in the tailpiece. Thread the other end through the peg hole, using tweezers if necessary. Clip off some of the excess length, leaving about 10 cm spare beyond the peg, and turn the peg so that the string winds towards the edge of the peg box, as shown in Fig. 37. If there is too much spare string, it may jam against the side of the peg box and make the peg difficult to turn. Gradually bring the string up to pitch, and keep retuning until it has settled.

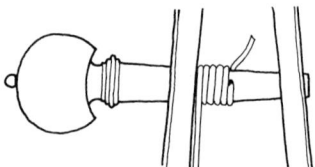

Fig. 37. A correctly wound string

## Wolf notes

The structure of viols causes certain frequencies (pitches) to resonate more strongly than others. Although this is often unnoticeable, it can sometimes cause certain notes to sound very unpleasant: these 'wolf' notes can be very dead (with no resonance) or very loud. In bad cases the note may warble and sound as if the bow is not gripping properly. On basses most wolf notes occur around the bottom G or F. On trebles and tenors they are most often found on the third string.

Unfortunately very little is known about the cause of this strange phenomenon, and it is hard to find a permanent cure. Adjusting the bridge, soundpost, or strings can help sometimes, or you can buy several types of wolf-note eliminator which helps to control it. A temporary but effective solution is to hold down a finger on the same note on a different string, or an octave higher or lower than the wolf note. The sympathetic resonance of this note improves the resonance of the wolf considerably. This is impractical in fast-moving passages but is certainly worthwhile on long notes. On a treble or tenor, where the bottom string is rarely played, you can tune that string an octave below the wolf, allowing it to vibrate in sympathy as described above.

A very bad wolf on a frequently used note can be most annoying, and could even be a reason for not buying a particular viol. However, even the very finest viols sometimes have wolf notes, so it is not necessarily a sign of a poor instrument.

*Frets*

Frets should be made of gut because, although unlike nylon it eventually wears out, it is more easily moved for tuning purposes and causes less wear on the strings. The frets should be graded in size, the thickest being at the nut and the thinnest towards the bridge. The top three strings of the viol provide a good guide to suitable thickness, and old strings can be used for replacing frets. If, as recommended by Simpson, you fit an octave fret, which can be a great help when playing in very high positions, you will have to use extremely thin gut or even thread, otherwise the top c♯″ will not sound.

Tying new frets is easy once you have learnt the knot; it may be as well to practise with bits of string and chair rungs first. The standard fret knot is shown in Fig. 38. Use a piece of gut at least 50–60 cm long to allow enough length for pulling the fret tight. Fold the gut in half and pass the loop under the strings and back round the neck, roughly in the position where the new fret is to be placed. Make another loop in one of the free ends and pass that through the first loop. Pass the other free end through the second loop as shown in the diagram and gradually pull the two ends tight. You will find you can get a tighter fit if you move the fret a little towards the nut when tying it. Once it is as tight as possible add one or two half hitches to secure the knot and then slide the fret to the correct position. The increase in thickness of the neck will tighten the fret still further. Finally trim the ends and sear them with a lighted match.

Unlike guitar frets, which are fixed permanently to the fingerboard, viol frets are movable. People often assume that, once a maker has put frets on a viol, they will never need to be moved again. But, however well in tune they may be originally, they will certainly not remain so, mainly because, as mentioned above, strings play sharper on the frets as they get older. You will find that you

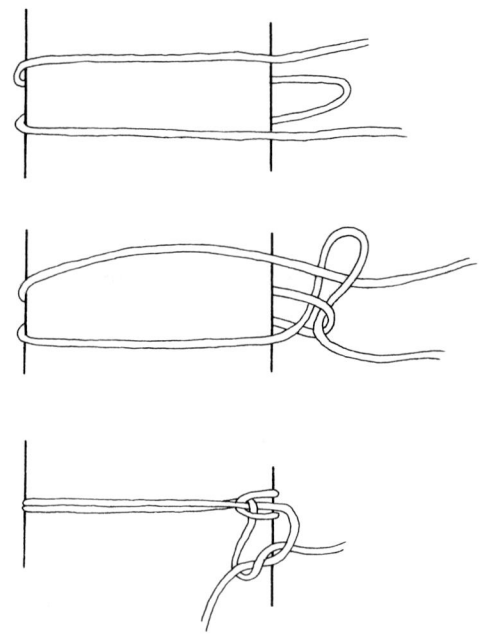

Fig. 38. The standard fret knot, viewed from behind the neck

have gradually to pull frets further back (towards the nut) to keep the tuning good. Due to different rates of wear on different strings, the ideal fret position may well vary with each string, in which case you will have to slope or bend the fret. Clearly this can only be taken to a certain point, and, when it becomes difficult to set the frets to achieve good intonation, it is time to change strings and readjust the frets accordingly. If you find it hard to judge the position of the frets by ear, use a tuning meter, or ask someone else to check them for you.

Frets are normally set in equal temperament, but they can also be adjusted to make tuning more pure, as described in Appendix 1.

## 5.3. Bows

Even if you can only afford a viol of moderate quality, a really good bow can make a great difference to your playing. Much of the advice given earlier about buying viols also applies to bows, and you will also need to choose a bow which suits your viol; some of the different types are shown in Fig. 39. If you have a

## 5.3. Bows 151

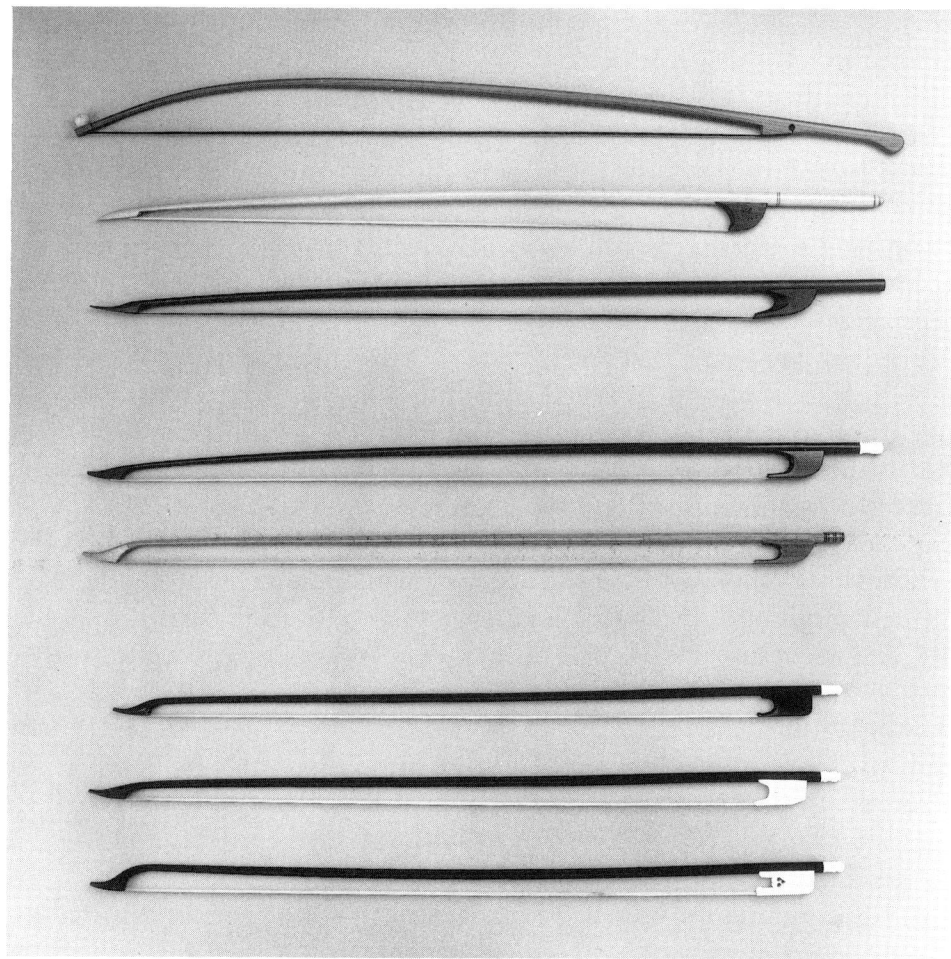

Fig. 39. Types of bow. (*from top to bottom*) 'Renaissance' bows by Christopher Allworth, Alan Crumpler, Ian Harwood; 'seventeenth-century' bows by Julian Clark, Doug Eaton; 'Baroque' bows by John Waterhouse, Sue Watt, John Waterhouse

Renaissance viol, an early 'stick'-type bow with a fixed frog and narrow hairing will be more suitable, but for most people a transitional or Baroque type is preferable. Normally these bows have a screw to adjust the tension, although some are available with a clip-in frog, which was more common in the seventeenth century.

The weight and length of a bow should relate to the size and type of viol; treble bows are lighter and slightly shorter than bass bows. A heavy bow generally produces a bigger sound, but one that is too heavy can stifle the resonance, especially in more lightly built instruments, which often sound better with a lighter bow. A very long bow is more difficult to control, while one that is too short can mean that you are continually running out of bow on long notes.

The strength and elasticity of the wood will greatly affect the feel of a bow. Most good bows are made of a hard wood such as pernambuco or snakewood, but even two apparently identical bows can react quite differently. The stick should flex slightly when you apply tension to the hair; it should neither be too stiff nor bend too easily. If you have small hands you may need to find a bow with a fairly shallow frog, otherwise you may have problems tensioning the hair with your middle finger.

When you buy a bow that is ready made or secondhand, you can try it out to see how it feels. If possible try several, taking one you like on approval, and ask advice from your teacher or an experienced player. If you order a bow from a maker, you can specify your requirements precisely, although you can never guarantee how the finished bow will feel.

Put enough rosin on the bow to enable it to grip the string well. You should see a little dust on the viol after playing for a while; if there is none you may not have used enough rosin. Use violin rather than cello rosin, which may be too sticky, and make sure it is of good quality—cheap rosin is very ineffective. Your rosin will last a long time if you keep turning it round to avoid wearing a groove down the middle.

Apply rosin firmly and pay particular attention to the playing (lower) edge of the hair and to the extreme tip of the bow, which often gets overlooked. Look along the hair to make sure that there are no shiny patches; you should be able to see rosin coming off when you flick the bow.

Every few months the bow hair will need cleaning to get rid of the buildup of rosin and also the grease that accumulates where the fingers touch the hair. Unscrew the frog completely, immerse the hair in a saucer of isopropyl alcohol or methylated spirit, and rub it gently with a strip of cotton rag or a toothbrush until it is clean. Be very careful not to splash spirit on the stick as it will spoil the finish. Alternatively use warm soapy water, but in this case be careful to rinse all the soap off afterwards.

Comb the hair to eliminate tangles and let it dry completely before replacing the frog. Remember that the bow will need much more rosin than usual after cleaning. Generally though, the danger to avoid is using too much rosin, which, as Forqueray (1767) says, can 'create a paste on the string, which makes it hiss and grate and dulls it'.

When a single strand of bow hair breaks, it is best to snip the broken ends off close with scissors rather than pull them, as this may loosen the rest of the hair. From time to time, depending on how much you play, the bow will need rehairing, because it will no longer grip even with adequate rosin. Also the hair may become too tight or too loose, or may lose too many strands. Rehairing is a professional job to be done by a bow maker or repairer.

The general rule on viols and bows is to buy the very best equipment you can afford and keep it in good playing order. This can make an enormous difference to the quality of your playing.

# Appendix 1. Tuning
## (by Elizabeth Liddle)

*Good intonation and pure intonation*

Good intonation is generally recognized by players and audiences, but it is a difficult thing to define precisely. Pure intervals can be defined precisely and mathematically, but intonation consisting entirely of intervals which are mathematically in tune is an ideal which is impossible to achieve on most instruments. Pure intervals are intervals found in the harmonic series, which is derived from the division of a sounding string length or column of air into whole-number ratios. This can be demonstrated easily on a viol: by touching a string lightly at the half-way point (1:2) and bowing it, a 'harmonic' one octave above the open string or 'fundamental' is produced; by touching the string at a point two-thirds along its length (2:3), a second harmonic, an octave and a fifth above the fundamental, is produced, and so on (Fig. 1). This series of harmonics is also present, although more faintly, when virtually any note is sounded on an instrument, and the relative proportions of the various harmonics present give a sound its characteristic quality.

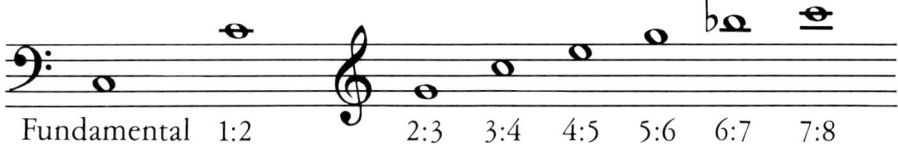

Fig. 1. The harmonic series (based on C string of bass viol)

When two identical notes are sounded together, the two sounds fuse into one. If the two notes differ slightly in pitch, 'beats' become audible, as the slightly different wavelengths move in and out of phase. The more out of tune the two notes are, the faster will be the beats, until the beats are no longer distinctly audible, but are perceived as a roughness of the sound. Eventually the two notes will be perceived as two separate pitches. Because low notes have lower frequencies than high notes, beats will be slower for a given amount of difference between two low notes than between two high notes. This may be a reason why an out-of-tune treble viol sounds more unpleasant than an out-of-tune bass.

Because of the series of harmonics present in most musical sounds, beats are also audible when you tune intervals other than a unison, most importantly the octave, the fifth, the fourth, and the major and minor thirds. This is because harmonics in common between the two pitches will beat together unless the interval is perfectly in tune. For example, when tuning the fourth between A and D, the harmonic two octaves above the A will coincide with the harmonic a twelfth above the D, and, unless the interval is perfectly in tune, these two sounds will beat against each other (Fig. 2).

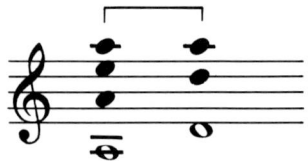

Fig. 2. Beating harmonics

Pure intervals, then, can be produced mathematically, by whole number ratios, and practically, by listening and adjusting until the beats between them disappear. However, because of the existence of 'commas' inherent in the mathematics of these pure musical intervals, problems arise for music composed in the Western tradition. For example, a chain of twelve absolutely pure fifths (or the inversion, fourths) starting on C (Fig. 3) ends on a B♯ which Western musical tradition often equates with C. It is, however, a little higher than C (about a quarter of a semitone), and this excess is called the Pythagorean comma.

Fig. 3. The Pythagorean comma

Similarly, a chain of four pure fifths or fourths (Fig. 4) exceeds the pure major third C–E by an amount known as the syntonic comma, which is just slightly smaller than the Pythagorean one. For most practical purposes we can regard these commas as being the same size.

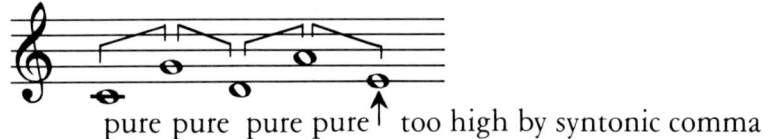

Fig. 4. The syntonic comma

## Tempering

Because of the existence of the Pythagorean comma, some or all of the fifths and fourths on any instrument have to be 'tempered'—deliberately made slightly impure—in order

Appendix 1. Tuning 157

to preserve the octave. But, because of the existence of the syntonic comma, we have an additional problem, in that in order to give good major thirds, the fifths and fourths have to be tempered still further. Generally speaking, when intervals are tempered, the fifths are narrowed, the fourths are widened, the major thirds are widened, and the minor thirds are narrowed.

The systems by which intervals are tempered are called temperaments. Each temperament is a compromise with its own advantages and disadvantages. Temperaments which are useful on the viol fall into three broad categories:

1. *Equal temperament*, in which the octave is divided into twelve equal semitones, and the fifths are all tempered by one-twelfth of a Pythagorean comma, allowing B♯ to equate exactly to C. One-twelfth of a comma is a very small alteration (about 2 cents, or two-hundredths of a semitone), so the fifths (and therefore the fourths) are very nearly pure. However, the major thirds, as a result of the existence of the syntonic comma, are two-thirds of a comma too wide (about 16 cents, or sixteen-hundredths of a semitone) and are therefore quite out of tune.
2. *Meantone temperaments*, in which there are two sizes of semitone. These temperaments address the problem posed by the syntonic comma. The fifths are tempered by a sizable fraction of a comma (e.g. a quarter-comma, a fifth-comma, or a sixth-comma). The resulting thirds are very good, although the fifths and fourths are tempered more heavily than modern ears are accustomed to. However, because the fifths and fourths are tempered by more than one-twelfth of the Pythagorean comma, enharmonics will not coincide, for example E♭ will not be the same pitch as D♯. On a keyboard instrument a decision has to be made as to which 'black notes' will serve for which enharmonic, and on a fretted instrument one of two possible fret positions has to be selected, hence the two sizes of semitone. The resulting temperament gives very good triads in the keys in which the correct enharmonics are available.
3. *Unequal circular temperaments*, in which each semitone is a different size, and the fifths and fourths are tempered by varying amounts. In effect, a compromise pitch is found for each enharmonic pair, in such a way as to give purer thirds in the simple keys at the expense of harsher thirds in the remote keys.

Setting temperaments on the viol is not as exact a science as on keyboard instruments. The nature of bowed sound means that pitch is not very precise, and varying bow pressure can alter pitch by a considerable amount. This means that the precise proportions of a comma by which each interval is tempered is less important than the prevention of an overall build-up of error leading to impure octaves and unisons, and glaringly wide major thirds.

However, the main problem with setting temperaments on the viol arises from the fact that each fret has to serve different notes on different strings. This means that, unless all the semitones are the same size, it is going to be difficult to place each fret so that it is correctly positioned for all the notes across the six (or seven) strings.

## Equal temperament

It follows, therefore, that the only temperament that can be reproduced without difficulty on the viol is equal temperament, as it is the only temperament in which all the semitones are of equal size and so the only temperament in which each fret can be placed so as to give a correct position on all strings.

The easiest way of setting frets to equal temperament is to use a piano or other pitch-source tuned in equal temperament. Tune the A string carefully to an A (or to a G♯ if you are playing at 415, or a G if at 392) on the piano. If you can hear beats, persevere until they are eliminated. Then set each fret carefully by ear to the respective notes on the piano or other pitch-source, making sure that the finger is placed behind the fret and not over it, so that the string is truly resonating from the fret. Then tune the D string to the pitch-source, and check that the frets are true for this string as well. You may need to 'bend' the frets slightly if your strings are old. (As a general rule, frets need to move towards the nut as the strings get older.) Then check all the other frets. If you have difficulty finding a fret position that works for all strings, you may need to renew your strings. When the frets are set and the viol is in tune, you will find that the fourths sound fairly pure, although they will be a little wider than pure by about 2 cents. On the bass, the beats will be very slow. The central major third, however, will be considerably wider than pure—about 16 cents, i.e. sixteen-hundredths of a semitone—and will beat fairly rapidly, even on the bass. To the ear accustomed to equal temperament, however, it will probably sound 'normal'.

With practice, it is possible to tune the fourths precisely and consistently, so that they are tempered by the correct small amount; the third is usually more difficult. It is, therefore, always worth checking the double octave between the outer strings in case the fourth string has been incorrectly tuned.

Because of its wide major thirds, equal temperament may be regarded as a rather out-of-tune temperament. This is a particular problem for a relatively unstable instrument such as the viol, and even more so for a whole consort of them, for the following reason: how well in tune a chord sounds is a function of the sum total of deviations from purity in its constituent intervals. In a temperament such as equal temperament, where the major thirds are already moderately out of tune, the ear's tolerance of any further deviation from purity caused by slipping pegs, changing humidity, etc., is very low. However, various unequal temperaments are possible that achieve purer major thirds at the expense of more heavily tempered fifths and fourths, and result in triads that have less total deviation from purity. This gives greater apparent stability to the tuning, as slight tuning inaccuracies are more tolerable in what is basically a better-tuned triad with a subjectively 'warmer' sound.

## Meantone temperaments

If the music to be played is in simple keys and does not modulate very far, a meantone fretting scheme may be adopted. The most extreme, and in many ways the most sonorous, form of meantone is 'quarter-comma meantone', in which each fifth is

# Appendix 1. Tuning

narrowed by a quarter of the syntonic comma (about $5\frac{1}{2}$ cents), resulting in a series of pure major thirds. Less extreme is fifth-comma meantone, in which each fifth is narrowed by a fifth of a comma (about $4\frac{1}{2}$ cents), resulting in major thirds which are only a fifth of a comma too wide.

A feature common to all meantone temperaments is that they create semitones of two different sizes, which generally alternate. As a simple rule, the first fret needs to be sharper than for equal temperament (nearer the bridge), the second flatter (nearer the nut), the third sharper, the fourth flatter, the fifth sharper, the sixth (usually) flatter, and the seventh sharper (Fig. 5a). The problems arise on the frets used for chromatic notes.

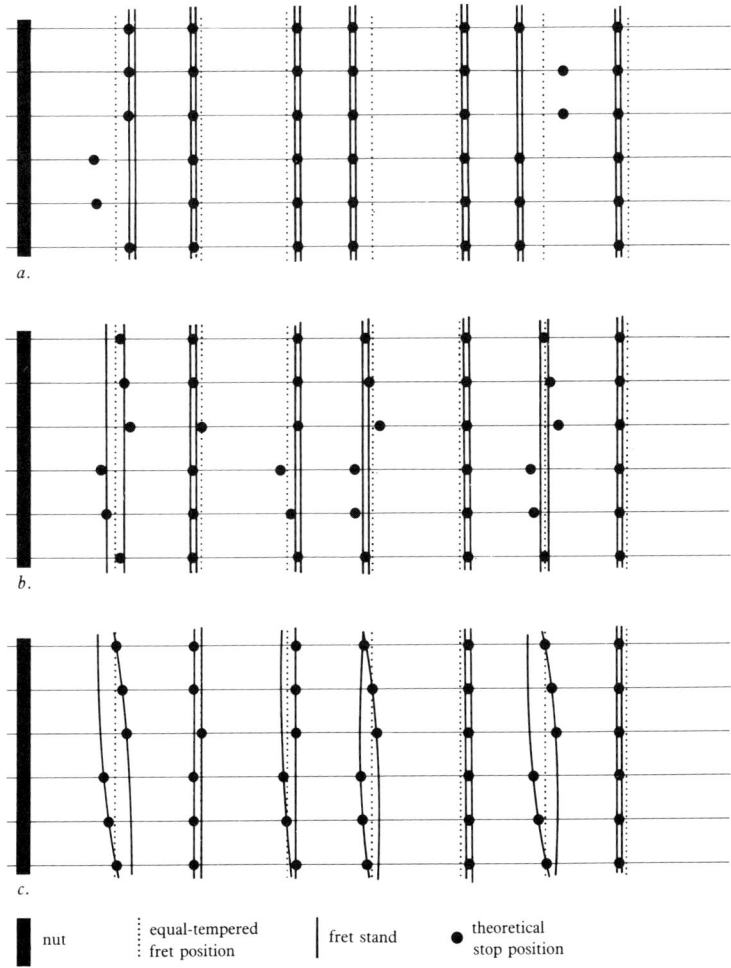

Fig. 5. Fretting schemes: *a.* for meantone temperament; *b.* for Vallotti's temperament; *c.* for Vallotti's temperament, using slanted, split frets. (For simplicity, the slight gradual diminution of fret spacing towards the bridge has been ignored.)

## Appendix 1. Tuning

The golden rule is that flats require the sharper fret position, and sharps require the flatter position. (It is important to remember this—many people think it is the other way round.) The most difficult problem this poses concerns the first fret. On the three upper strings the fret is generally used for flats, and so should be in the sharper position. However, on the fourth and fifth strings it is generally used for sharps, and so needs to be in the flatter position. If the fret is placed in the sharper position, the problem of intonation on the fourth and fifth strings may escape notice in fast passages. In slow passages it is sometimes possible to finger these notes on the sixth fret of the string below. However, it is often worthwhile to separate the two strands of the fret, so that the nut-side strand can be used for the sharps, and the bridge-side strand for the flats. This arrangement not only allows for a good low D♯ on the top string (bass and treble) in E minor, but also provides a good high E♭ on the same string.

To set frets in meantone temperament, it is useful to have a tuning meter. Table 1 gives the deviations in cents from equal temperament for each note in quarter-comma, fifth-comma, and sixth-comma meantone. It does not matter if you do not get a very exact reading for every note, but by keeping to the table you will ensure that notes

TABLE 1. Unequal temperaments, deviation from equal temperament, in cents

|     | Quarter-comma meantone | Fifth-comma meantone | Sixth-comma meantone | Valotti |
|-----|---|---|---|---|
| A♯  | −24.5 | −17.5 | −14 | +6 |
| D♯  | −21   | −15   | −12 | +4 |
| G♯  | −17.5 | −12.5 | −10 | +2 |
| C♯  | −14   | −10   | −8  | 0  |
| F♯  | −10.5 | −7.5  | −6  | −2 |
| B   | −7    | −5    | −4  | −4 |
| E   | −3.5  | −2.5  | −2  | −2 |
| A   | 0     | 0     | 0   | 0  |
| D   | +3.5  | +2.5  | +2  | +2 |
| G   | +7    | +5    | +4  | +4 |
| C   | +10.5 | +7.5  | +6  | +6 |
| F   | +14   | +10   | +8  | +8 |
| B♭  | +17.5 | +12.5 | +10 | +6 |
| E♭  | +21   | +15   | +12 | +4 |
| A♭  | +24.5 | +17.5 | +14 | +2 |
| D♭  | +28   | +20   | +16 | 0  |

One cent is 1/100th of an equal tempered semitone, i.e. 1/1200th of an octave. If you have a tuning meter which shows cents, you should tune each note sharp or flat by the amount in cents shown in this table.

*Appendix 1. Tuning* 161

remote from each other on the table bear the right sort of relationship to each other. Once the frets are set, tuning can be done by ear, and the open strings checked so that they make a good unison with the stopped note on the string below. (Only do this if the frets have been recently checked.) It takes a while to learn to gauge the sound of the rather heavily tempered fourths, but the central third is easier, as it should be absolutely pure in quarter-comma meantone, and only slightly wider than pure in the less extreme meantone temperaments.

A viol consort accurately tuned in quarter-comma meantone sounds especially sonorous, as the pure major thirds give a special warmth to the sound. However the temperament can appear unstable. Because the fifths and fourths are as heavily tempered as the ear can bear, any further deviation from purity can be unacceptable. Furthermore, the difference between enharmonics (e.g. D♯/E♭) is quite large, and can be difficult to negotiate in chromatic passages, or remote keys. Fifth-comma meantone is a good compromise for unstable climatic conditions, and can sound almost as good. Sixth-comma meantone is a possibility for more chromatic music.

## Unequal circular temperaments

For tonally adventurous music, where the meantone temperaments start to pose greater problems than they solve, the unequal circular temperaments are a much more exciting solution than equal temperament. In the simple keys they have the characteristic good thirds of meantone temperaments, and, while they are more strident than equal temperament in the remoter keys, the specific character of each key can enhance enjoyment of both listening and playing. Because, in these temperaments, a compromise pitch is found for enharmonics, enharmonic modulations where, for example, a D♯ is tied to an E♭ in the next chord, is possible.

However, because all such temperaments involve several different sizes of semitone, considerable problems are presented for fretted instruments. Further problems arise because, unlike equal or meantone temperaments, in which all the fifths and fourths are identical, most unequal circular temperaments involve a variety of fifths and fourths. Because viols are tuned largely in fourths, only temperaments in which all the open-string fourths are identical are really feasible, as only in these temperaments will at least a few straight fret positions be possible.

One unequal circular temperament that fulfils this criterion is Vallotti's in which the six 'white-note' fifths are tempered by a sixth of a comma, and the remaining fifths (those which include a 'black note') are tuned pure. The resulting fretting scheme is shown in Fig. 5b.

As can be seen, the positions for frets two, three, five, and seven are similar to those for a meantone system. The remaining frets are placed in compromise positions, as their ideal position would be in a sort of Z shape. However, I find that very good intonation on these frets can be achieved if:

1. The frets are fairly thick, and so notes that need to be sharpened can be raised by pressing the string in behind the fret (Fig. 6).

## 162  Appendix 1. Tuning

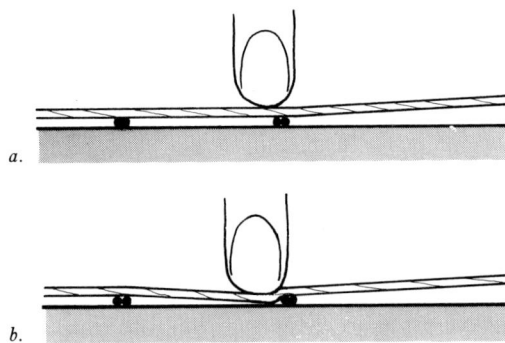

Fig. 6. Position of finger in relation to fret
    *a.* for flattest possible note
    *b.* for sharpest possible note

2. It is remembered that the basic pattern of intonation is the same for each of these frets (and also to a certain extent for fret three), so that, from the top string down to the third string, the notes should be stopped steadily sharper on each string, the sharpest note being played on the third string. The fourth string is then stopped very flat, the fifth slightly less flat, and the sixth the same as the first.

In practice, I find that the only real difficulty is in achieving both a sharp enough F (bass and treble) or B♭ (tenor) on the third string, first fret, and a flat enough C♯ (bass and treble) or F♯ (tenor) on the fourth string, first fret, and that this difficulty can be overcome, as with the meantone fretting scheme, by a small separation of the strands of the first fret. In any case, if these frets are placed at a slight slant and a little separated (Fig. 5c), all the theoretical fret positions are readily obtainable.

Table 1 gives the deviations in cents from equal temperament for Vallotti's temperament. Once the frets are set, the tuning is fairly easy but, as with all temperaments, takes practice. The open strings are in fact tuned as for sixth-comma meantone. The fourths should be a little wider than for equal temperament, but not as wide as for quarter-comma meantone. The open-string major third should be a little wider than pure, but narrower than for equal temperament.

### General rules for unequal temperaments

It may be seen, therefore, that the adjustment of frets away from their equal-temperament positions follows the same general pattern for both meantone and Vallotti, and this is true of most unequal temperaments. A few basic rules can therefore be made that govern the tempering of open strings and the placing of frets:

1. When tuning open strings, the fourths should always be a little wider than pure.
2. The narrower (purer) the open-string major third, the wider must be the fourths between the remaining strings, and the less equal will be the resulting temperament.

3. In order to keep the unisons and octaves between open strings and fretted notes pure, the following fret adjustments are required for unequal temperaments:
   Fret two must move flatter (i.e. towards the nut)
   Fret three must move sharper (i.e. towards the bridge)
   Fret five must move sharper
   Fret seven must move flatter
4. The remaining frets must be adjusted empirically, to achieve either a self-consistent meantone fretting or a workable circular temperament.

## *Tuning a consort*

To achieve good intonation in consort playing it is clearly essential that the temperament for each viol should be the same. For a group that plays together regularly, therefore, it is worth setting the frets together according to an instrument that has previously been set to a self-consistent temperament. If this is not feasible, it is none the less essential that open strings be tuned identically on all instruments. Fretted notes can be modified by the left hand or the fret corrected empirically, as you go along.

As there is a tendency for the ear to perceive tuning from the bass, it is sensible to tune the bass of the consort first, checking octaves between fretted notes and open strings. The double octave between top and bottom strings can be checked more easily by bowing the bottom string while simultaneously plucking the top string with the left hand. The bass can then give notes to the rest of the consort, checking periodically that it itself is not changing. In unstable conditions it is sometimes best to give all the notes from the second, third, and fourth strings, and then to recheck the lower strings again at the end as they are more liable to change. For the tenor F string, give the F on the E string, first sounding it with the open C to check that it makes a good fourth.

When all the viols have been tuned, it is a good idea to start with a slow piece in a good key, say a pavan in G major. Stop at any bad-sounding chords and check the tuning as follows:

1. Check that the bass is still in tune with itself.
2. Check that all unisons and octaves with the bass in the chord are pure; if not, check the open string, then adjust the fret if necessary.
3. Check that the fifths and fourths with the bass are tempered in accordance with the temperament used; check the open string first, then the fret. Remember: narrow fifths, wide fourths, although they should always sound acceptable.
4. Add the third of the chord, checking the open string first, then the fret. Even if the third is not very pure, if the rest of the chord is good it will probably sound acceptable.

Once your ears are accustomed to good intonation, it will become possible in many cases to 'pull' chords into completely pure or 'just' intonation, for example on final cadences. The fifths can be sharpened a little by pulling the string slightly sideways or pressing harder behind the fret, and the major thirds flattened if necessary, by reducing the pressure of the left-hand finger on the string. As it is easier to sharpen notes with the left hand than to flatten them, frets should be placed so that they are in the flattest position required. An open string can be raised in pitch temporarily, for example on the final chord of a piece, by pressing behind the nut with the first finger.

## *Playing with a keyboard instrument*

If you are playing with an organ or harpsichord, it is desirable to discuss temperament with the player beforehand and arrange a suitable scheme for the music. In any case, it is essential to tune the open strings to the keyboard, and then to adjust the frets to give acceptable unisons. For consorts playing with organ, meantone temperaments often work well, although the organ will not have the optional enharmonics that are possible with split frets on the viols. When playing with a harpsichord in an unequal temperament, it is worth asking for a temperament that is relatively easy to reproduce on the viol, e.g. Vallotti, or a meantone temperament. Others, such as Werckmeister II, may be difficult to reproduce precisely and more split frets may be necessary. Always remember that thicker frets allow for more flexibility in tuning.

## *Playing with a lute*

Lute players are understandably more reluctant than viol players to depart from equal temperament, partly because the pitch of the lute is more difficult to 'bend' with the left hand, and partly because the short decay time of a plucked note makes the high major thirds of equal temperament more acceptable. Eighth-comma meantone (fifths and fourths tempered by about 3 cents, major thirds enlarged by about 11 cents) is a possible compromise. For the viols to play in a slightly more extreme meantone temperament than the lute often proves surprisingly successful, provided that the viols tune to a note from the lute that is the keynote of the piece to be played, and that the piece does not modulate too far afield.

# Appendix 2. Useful Addresses (UK and USA)

## SOCIETIES

Viola da Gamba Society of Great Britain
56 Hunters Way, Dringhouses, York YO2 2JJ
Viola da Gamba Society of America Inc.
253 E. Delaware, Apt. 12F, Chicago, IL 60611
Early Music America
1141½ Bellflower Road, Cleveland, OH 44106
Viola da Gamba
Gesellschaft, Möttelistr. 1, CH-8400 Winterhur, Switzerland

## JOURNALS

Early Music, Oxford University Press
70 Baker Street, London W1M 1DJ
Early Music News
3 Onslow House, Castle Road, The Common, Tunbridge Wells, Kent TN4 8BY

## ENGLISH DEALERS

Bridgewood and Neitzert (strings and repairs)
146 Stoke Newington Church Street, London N16 0UH

Brian Jordan (music, books, and facsimiles)
10 Green Street, Cambridge CB2 3JU

The Cambridge Music Shop
All Saints Passage, Cambridge CB2 3LT

The Early Music Shop
38 Manningham lane, Bradford, West Yorkshire BD1 3EA

Northern Renaissance Instruments (and strings)
6 Needham Avenue, Chorlton, Manchester M21 2AA

## AMERICAN DEALERS

Boulder Early Music Shop
2010 Fourteenth Street, Boulder, Colorado 80302
Early Music Shop of New England
59 Boylston Street, Brookline, Ma 02146, USA
The Provincetown Bookshop Inc.
246 Commercial Street, Provincetown, Ma 02657, USA
Damian Dlugolecki (strings)
520 SE 40th St. #5E, Troudale, Oregon 97060-2568, USA
Daniel Larson (strings)
267 N. 28th Ave. E., Duluth, MN 55812, USA

# Appendix 3. Published Music for the Viol

The following is not a complete list, but a selection of publications including most areas of the solo and ensemble repertoire. The sections are divided by country of origin, type of music, and composer. Publication dates are given wherever available.

### ENGLISH

*Consort Music*

Brade, William, *Pavans, Galliards & Canzonas 1609* (5 parts; London Pro Musica, 1982).
Byrd, William, *Consort Music* (3–6 viols; The Byrd Edition, 17; Stainer and Bell, London, 1973; score only).
—— *Consort Songs* (voice and 4 viols; The Byrd Edition, 16; Stainer and Bell, London, 1973; score only).
—— *Consort Music* (4 vols. for 3–6 viols; Northwood Music, Urbana, Illinois, 1986).
—— *10 Consort Songs* (voice and 4 viols; Corda Music, St Albans, 1987).
—— *Consort Songs* (voice and 4 viols with lute ad lib; Fretwork Editions, Richmond, Surrey, 1990).
Coprario, Giovanni, *Consort Music in 6 parts* (Boethius, Kilkenny, 1982).
—— *Five-Part Consort Music* (3 vols., Golden Phoenix, Corda Music, St Albans, 1989).
—— *Complete Two-, Three- and Four-Part Consort Music* (Fretwork Editions, 1991).
Dowland, John, *Lachrimae* (5 viols and lute; Oxford University Press, 1927; facsimile Boethius, Kilkenny, 1974; Schott, London 1985).
—— *First Book of Songs* (Golden Phoenix, Harpenden, 1986).
—— *The Second Book of Songs or Ayres* (a set of 6 part-books, Corda Music, St Albans, 1990).
Ferrabosco, Alfonso, *4-part Fantasies* (some with 2 trebles; English Consort Series, 4 and 5; Early Music Centre Publications, London, 1978).
——Complete 6 part Consort Music (3 vols., Corda Music, St Albans, 1990).
Gibbons, Orlando, *Nine 3-part Fantasies* (English Consort Series, 19; Early Music Centre Publications, London, 1981).
—— *Fantasies in 6 parts* (with organ; Faber Music, London, 1982).
—— *Consort Music for 2–6 viols*, in 5 vols. (Northwood Music, Urbana, Illinois, 1983).
Hingeston, John, *Fantasies and Airs* (3 bass viols; Dovehouse, 38, Canada, 1983).
—— *Suites for 3 to 6 viols* (4 vols, PRB productions, 1991–95).
Holborne, Anthony, *Pavans, Galliards & Almains 1599* (5 parts; London Pro Musica, 1980; facsimile; Grage, West Germany).

Jenkins, John, *Seven Fancies* (3 viols; Hortus Musicus, 149; Bärenreiter, Kassel, 1957).
—— *Newark Siege* (2 trebles and 2 basses; Viola da Gamba Society, 25, London, 1966).
—— *Consort Music of 4 Parts* (with violins; Musica Britannica, 26; Stainer and Bell, London, 1967; score only).
—— *Consort Music in Five Parts* (Faber Music, London, 1971).
—— *Consort Music in Six Parts* (Faber Music, London, 1976).
—— *Consort Music in Four Parts* (Faber Music, London, 1978).
Lawes, William, *Fantasia Suites* (2 vols; 1/2 violins, bass viol and organ; Stainer and Bell, London 1991).
—— *Consort Sets in 5 and 6 Parts* (with organ; Faber Music, London, 1979).
—— *Two Suites* (2 trebles and 2 basses; Dovehouse, Canada, 1983).
Locke, Matthew, *Six Suites* (3 viols; Hortus Musicus, 180; Bärenreiter, Kassel, 1964).
—— *The Flat Consort* (3 viols; Stainer and Bell, London, 1971).
—— *Consort Music in 4 Parts* (Stainer and Bell, London, 1972).
—— *The Little Consort* (3 viols; Golden Phoenix, Harpenden, 1986).
Lupo, Thomas, *Consort Music in 2, 3, and 4 parts* (2 vols., Boethius, Kilkenny, 1983, 1988).
—— *The Six-Part Consort Music* (Fretwork Editions, London, 1993).
Mico, Richard, *Consort Music in 2 to 5 Parts* (2 vols., Stainer and Bell, London, 1994).
Purcell, Henry, *15 Fantasies and In nomines* (3–7 viols/violins; Novello, London, 1969, Northwood Music, Illinois, 1995).
Simpson, Christopher, *22 Dances* (2 trebles, bass and continuo; Dovehouse, 17, Canada, 1981).
—— *The Months* (treble and 2 basses; Dovehouse, 31, Canada, 1982).
Tomkins, Thomas, *Six-part Fantasies* (Northwood Music, Urbana, Illinois, 1987).
—— *Complete Consort Music for 3–6 viols*, in 2 vols. (Stainer and Bell, 1991).
Ward, John, *Four-Part Fantasias and In nomines* (4 vols., PRB, California, 1992–3).
—— *Fantasias in 5 and 6 parts* (Northwood Music, Illinois, 1994; Stainer and Bell, London, 1995).
Various, *In nomines* (4–5 viols; Hortus Musicus, 134; Bärenreiter, Kassel, 1974).
—— *Elizabethan Consort Music* (3–6 parts; Musica Britannica, 44–45; Stainer and Bell, London, 1979; score only).

Numerous other works by seventeenth-century English composers are published by the Viola da Gamba Society, including some in facsimile, and by Early Music Centre Publications, Northwood Music, PRB, and Dovehouse.

## Divisions

Anon., *Divisions* (unaccompanied, several vols; Viola da Gamba Society, 137, 139, 140, London, 1980–1).
Jenkins, John, *Divisions in D minor* (violin, bass and continuo; Schott, London, 1958).
—— *Airs & Divisions* (2 basses and keyboard; Dovehouse, 7, Canada, 1979).

Lawes, William, *Suites for Division Viols* (2 basses and organ; Viola da Gamba Society, London, 1974, also in Musica Britannica, 21—see above).
Simpson, Christopher, *The Division Viol* (1665; fascimile; Faber Music, London).
—— *Divisions in G* (with keyboard; Dovehouse, 11, Canada, 1980).
Dovehouse publish a number of other English divisions, mostly for two basses.

## Duets

Carolo [Mr], *Sonatas 1–6* (2 basses and keyboard; Golden Phoenix, Harpenden, 1986).
Coprario, Giovanni, *12 Fantasies* (2 basses and keyboard; Dovehouse, Canada, 1979).
—— *Six Fantasies* (treble and tenor; Northwood Music, Urbana, Illinois, 1982).
Gibbons, Orlando, *Six Fantasies* (2 trebles; Heinrichshofen, Wilhelmshaven, 1970).
Hely, Benjamin, *Six Suites* (2 basses and continuo; King's Music, London, 1980).
Hingeston, John, *Four Fantasies* (2 basses; Nova Music, Brighton).
Locke, Matthew, *Duos* (2 basses; King's Music, London, 1981).
Mico, Richard, *Four Fantasies* (treble and bass; Ogni Sorte Editions, Ottawa, 1978).
Morley, John, *Nine Fantasies* (2 trebles/treble and tenor; Hortus Musicus, 136, Bärenreiter, Kassel, 1956).
Ward, John, *Six Airs* (2 basses and keyboard; Dovehouse, 5, Canada, 1979).
Withy, John, *Treble & Bass of a Ground* (treble and bass; facsimile; Viola da Gamba Society, 94, London, 1972).
Dovehouse publish a number of other English duet volumes.

## Lyra viol

Coprario, Giovanni, *11 Pieces for 3 Lyra Viols* (A–R Editions).
Corkine, William, *The Second Book of Ayres* (includes some songs with lyra viol; English Lute Songs in Facsimile; Scolar Press, London, 1970).
Ferrabosco, Alfonso, *Lessons for 1, 2 & 3 Lyra Viols* (facsimile; Theatrum Orbis Terrarum, Amsterdam, 1973).
Ford, Thomas, *Musicke of Sundrie Kinds* (2 lyra viols; English Lute Songs in Facsimile; Scolar Press, London, 1966).
Hume, Tobias, *The First Part of Ayres, French, Polish & Others* (1605; 1, 2, and 3 lyra viols; English Lute Songs in Facsimile; Scolar Press, London, 1969).
—— *Captain Hume's Poeticall Musick* (1607; including some songs with lyra viol; English Lute Songs in Facsimile; Scolar Press, London, 1970).
Sumarte, Richard, *Solos for Lyra Viol* (Viola da Gamba Society, 102, London, 1974).
Various, *Music for the Lyra Viol* (Chiltern Music, Chichester, 1983).
—— *Tablature for One* (Bishop, Atlanta, 1982).
—— *Tablature for Two* (Bishop, Atlanta, 1980).
—— *Tablature for Three* (Bishop, Atlanta, 1980).

## SPANISH AND ITALIAN

### Chamber Music

Corelli, Arcangelo, *Two Sonatas* (facsimile; bass and continuo, transcribed from violin sonatas; Viola da Gamba Society, 136, London, 1980).

Fontana, Giovanni Battista, *Sonatas* (violin, bass and continuo; Doblinger; Diletto Musicale, 1962).

Frescobaldi, Girolamo, *Canzonas for Bass Instrument and Continuo* (London Pro Musica, GF2, 1979).

—— *Canzonas for Treble Instrument and Continuo* (London Pro Musica, CF1, 1975).

Merula, Tarquinio, *Canzonas a 4* (Dovehouse, Canada, 1983).

Ruffo, Vincenzo, *4 Pieces* (3 viols; London Pro Musica, IM2, 1972).

—— *Capriccii in musica 1564* (3 parts; facsimile; Studio per Edizioni Scelte, Florence, 1979).

*Seven Instrumental Pieces from Petrucci's Canti C* (London Pro Musica, AN3, 1981).

### Divisions

Dalla Casa, Girolamo, *Madrigali e canzoni* (2 vols.; bass and lute or keyboard; partly facsimile; London Pro Musica, REP 4 and 6, 1980–1).

Ganassi, Sylvestro di, *Regola rubertina* (unaccompanied; partly facsimile; Peters, London, 1977).

Ortiz, Diego, *Tratado de glosas* (mostly with continuo; Bärenreiter, Kassel, 1936; Heugel, Paris, 1978).

Rognoni, Francesco, *Viola bastarda settings* (London Pro Musica, REP 9, 1986).

Virgiliano, Aurelio, *Three Ricercadas* (unaccompanied; London Pro Musica, REP 2, 1980).

London Pro Musica, Dovehouse, and Studio per Edizioni Scelte publish many other volumes of Italian instrumental and vocal music suitable for viols.

## GERMAN AND AUSTRIAN

### Solo sonatas and duets

Abel, Karl Friedrich, *Sonata in G* (unaccompanied; Schott, London, 1953).

—— *Six Sonatas* (unaccompanied; Dovehouse, Canada, 1982).

—— *Six Sonatas* (treble or bass and continuo; 2 vols.; Hortus Musicus, 39/40; Bärenreiter, Kassel, 1968).

—— *Twelve Sonatas from the Countess of Pembroke's Music Book* (2 vols., Asclepius Editions, Malvern, 1995–6).

Bach, Carl Philipp Emanuel, *Sonata in G minor* (bass and obbligato keyboard; Schott, Mainz, 1969).
—— *Sonata in D* (Peters, Leipzig, 1933).
Bach, Johann Sebastian, *Neue Bach Ausgabe* (Bärenreiter, Kassel, 1984).
—— *Three Sonatas* (bass and obbligato harpsichord; Faber Music, London, 1987).
Buxtehude, Dietrich, *Sonata* (Schott, London, 1956).
Finger, Godfrey, *Sonatina* (2 basses; Dovehouse, 18, Canada, 1980).
—— *Two Suites* (2 basses; Dovehouse, 24, Canada, 1981).
—— *Sonatas 2 & 4* (Dovehouse, 40, Canada, 1983).
Handel, Georg Frideric, *Sonata in G minor* (Schott, London, 1950).
—— *Sonata in C* (doubtful attribution; bass and obbligato harpsichord; Hortus Musicus, 112; Bärenreiter, Kassel, 1953).
Kuhnel, August, *Sonata o Partite 1698* (1/2 basses and optional continuo; facsimile; Musica, Peer, Belgium, 1984).
Schenk, Johann, *Suite in A* from *Scherzi musicali* (Hortus Musicus; Bärenreiter, Kassel, 1963).
—— *Le Nymphe di Rheno* (6 sonatas for 2 basses; Das Erbe Deutscher Musik, 44; Nagels Verlag, Kassel, 1956; facsimile; Minkoff, Geneva, 1995).
—— *L'Echo du Danube* (6 sonatas; Das Erbe Deutscher Musik, 67; Nagels Verlag, Kassel, 1973; facsimile, Minkoff, Geneva, 1993).
—— *Scherzi musicali* (facsimile; Société de Musicologie du Languedoc, Beziers, 1983).
—— *Tyd en Kunst Oeffeningen* (1688; facsimile; Musica, Peer, Belgium, 1986).
Telemann, Georg Philipp, *Sonata in A minor* (Peters, Leipzig).
—— *Sonata in E minor* (Peters, Leipzig).
—— *Sonata in G* (treble or bass and continuo; Hortus Musicus, 189; Bärenreiter, Kassel, 1965).
—— *Sonata in D* (unaccompanied; Schott, London, 1970).
—— *Esercizii musici* (facsimile; includes solo and trio sonatas; Musica Musica, Basle).
—— *Der getreue Musikmeister* (1728; facsimile; includes solo and trio sonatas; Musica Musica, Basle, 1980).

*Ensemble Music*

Buxtehude, Dietrich, *Six Trio Sonatas* (violin, bass and continuo; Bärenreiter, Kassel, 1957).
Nicolai, Johann Michael, *Two Sonatas* (3 basses and continuo; Dovehouse, 34, Canada, 1981).
Schmelzer, Johann Heinrich, *Trio Sonatas* (violin, bass and continuo; Akademische Druck, Graz, 1976).
Schwarzkopff, Theodor, *Suite* (treble, bass and continuo; Dovehouse, Canada).
Telemann, George Philipp, various trio sonatas in Esercizii Musici and Der Getreue Musikmeister (see above) and in modern editions.

—— *Paris Quartets* (flute, violin, bass, and continuo; facsimile; 2 vols. of 6 quartets each, Musica Musica, Basle; *Quartets 1–6* (Bärenreiter, Kassel, 1965–8).

## Orchestral Music/Cantatas

Bach, Johann Sebastian, *Les Airs pour viole de gambe* (extracts from the Passions and cantatas; Zurfluh, Paris, 1984).

Buxtehude, Dietrich, *Jubilate Domino* (alto, bass viol, and continuo; Bärenreiter, Kassel, 1974).

Telemann, Georg Philipp, *Concerto in E* (violin, bass viol, and harpsichord; Peters, London 1927).

—— *Concerto in A minor* (recorder, bass viol, and strings; Moeck, Celle, 1960).


### FRENCH

## Solos, suites, and duets

(for bass viol and continuo unless otherwise stated)

Boismortier, Joseph Bodin de, *Suites* (facsimile; Minkoff, Geneva).

—— *Six sonates* (2 basses; Heugel, Paris, 1975; facsimile; Kings Musick, 1995).

—— *Petites Sonates* (2 basses; facsimile; Oxford University Press, London, 1983).

Caix d'Hervelois, Louis de, *Premier Livre de pièces de viole avec la basse continue* (facsimile; Caldwell, Oberlin, Ohio, 1972).

—— *Troisième livre 1731* (facsimile; Zurfluh, Paris, 1974).

—— *Deuxième suite* (treble/pardessus and continuo; Dovehouse, 19, Canada, 1980).

Couperin, François, *Pièces de viole* (1728; facsimile, Minkoff, Geneva, 1986; Heugel, Paris).

—— *Concerts* (1724; 2 basses; facsimile; Zurfluh, Paris, 1981).

Couperin, Louis, *Pièces pour les violes* (2 fantasies, 3 symphonies for 1 and 2 viols and continuo; Pièces de Clavecin, Éditions de l'Oiseau-Lyre).

Dollé, Charles, *Variés pièces de viole* (Heugel, Paris).

Forqueray, Antoine, *Pièces de viole* (Guilys, Fribourg, 1984; facsimile, Broude Brothers, New York).

Heudeline, Louis, *Suite* (from the *Premier livre*; treble and continuo; Dovehouse, 41, Canada, 1984).

Hotteterre, Jacques, *Suites for Treble Viol* (Nova Music, Brighton, 1979–80).

Marais, Marin, *Pièces de viole* (1689, 1701, 1711, 1717, 1725; some for 2 basses and continuo; 5 vols.; facsimile; Schola Cantorum Basiliensis, Basle, 1982).

—— *Pièces de viole* (critical edition by John Hsu; Broude Brothers, New York, 1980–6)

—— *Suite* (from the *Quatrième livre*; Associated Music Publishers, New York, 1974).

—— *Suite* (from the *Cinquième livre*; Heugel, Paris, 1977).

—— *Six Suites* (from the *Troisième* and *Quatrième* livres; A–R Editions, Madison, Wisconsin, 1976).

Machy, Le Sieur de, *Pièces de violes* (Dovehouse, Canada; facsimile; Minkoff, Geneva, 1973).
Marc, Thomas, *Suite de pièces* (treble/pardessus and continuo; Dovehouse, 29, Canada, 1982).
Sainte Colombe, —— *Suites* (2 basses; Minkoff, Geneva).
Minkoff, Fuzeau, and SPES publish many other facsimile volumes of French music.

## Ensemble Music

Corrette, Michel, *Le Phénix* (3/4 basses and optional continuo; Carus-Verlag, Stuttgart, 1976).
Couperin, François, *Les Nations*, (1726; with violin, flute, or other instruments; facsimile; Musica Musica, Basle, 1982).
—— *Trio Sonatas* (Musica Rara, London, 1976; facsimile, Minkoff, Geneva, 1979).
—— *Concerts royaux* (Musica Rara, London, 1976).
Hotteterre, Jacques, *Première suite de pièces* (2 trebles; facsimile; Musica Musica, Basle).
Marais, Marin, *La Gamme et autres morceaux de simphonie* (1723 violin, bass and continuo; facsimile; Musica Musica, Basle).
—— *Sonnerie de Ste Geneviève du Mont de Paris* (1723; facsimile; UCP Publications, Paris).
—— *Pièces en trio* (1692; 2 trebles and continuo; facsimile; Studio per Edizioni Scelte, Florence, 1982).
Rameau, Jean-Philippe, *Pièces de clavecin en concert* (harpsichord with violin/flute and bass; Bärenreiter, Kassel, 1976; facsimile, JM Fuzeau, Courlay, France).

### TWENTIETH-CENTURY MUSIC

Ballinger, Peter, *Trio* (treble, tenor, bass; PRB Productions).
Benjamin, George, *Upon Silence* (5 viols and mezzo/alto; Faber, 1990).
Bishop, Martha, *Elegy and Passacaglia* (tenor and two bass viols; PRB Productions).
Briars, Gavin, *In Nomine* (6 viols; Schott, 1995).
Fricker, Peter Racine, *Elegy. The Tomb of St Eulalia* (countertenor, bass viol, and harpsichord; Schott, London, 1956).
Guy, Barry, *Buzz* (5 viols; Novello, 1995).
Joubert, John, *Tombeau* (unaccompanied; Nova Music, London, 1981).
Loeb, David, *Nine fantasias for the Japanese Consort* (PRB Productions).
Pallis, Marco, *Divisions on a Ground* (6 sets, 2 for treble, 4 for bass; Thames Publishing, London 1980).
Ridout, Alan, *Tombeau de M. Alfred Deller* (unaccompanied).
Tcherepnin, Alexander, *Sonata da Chiesa* (Simrock, 1969).
Volans, Kevin, *White Man Sleeps* (bass viol, 2 harpsichords, and percussion; Newer music edition, 1984).

PRB Productions (Albany, Ca. USA) publish several other new pieces for viols.

*Appendix 3. Published Music for the Viol*

ANTHOLOGIES

Crum, A. (ed.), *First Solos* (3 vols. for treble, tenor, bass; Corda Music, 1996).
Crum, A. (ed.), *Intermediate Solos* (3 vols. for treble, tenor, bass; Corda Music, 1996).
Matiffa, E. (ed.), *Pièces faciles* (De Machy, Marais, and others; Heugel, Paris, 1976).
Bloch (ed.), *Pièces faciles des 16 et 17 siècles* (Arwen, Riaille, France, 1979).
Pallis, M. (ed.), *Renaissance Tunes* (7 vols.; Thames Publishing, London, 1984).

STUDIES AND SCALES

Bishop, Martha, *40 Melodic and Progressive Exercises for Viola da Gamba* (treble, tenor, bass; Bishop, Atlanta, 1982–3).
—— *Scales* (treble, tenor, bass; Bishop, Atlanta, 1982).
—— *Vade mecum: Daily Exercises for Bass Viol* (Bishop, Atlanta, 1981).
Schwamberger, K. M. (ed.), *Ubungen* (Rahter, Hamburg, 1965).
Langin F. (ed.), *Gamben Studien* (extracts from original works; Breitkopf and Härtel, Wiesbaden, 1968).

# Bibliography

### TREATISES REFERRED TO IN THE TEXT

Dalla Casa, G. (1584): *Il vero modo di diminuir* (facsimile; Forni).
Danoville, —(1687): *L'Art de toucher le dessus et basse de violle* (facsimile; Minkoff, Geneva).
Forqueray, J.-B. (1767): Letters to Friedrich Wilhelm of Prussia (English trans. in *Journal of the Viola da Gamba Society of America*, 13 (1976)).
Ganassi, S. (1542–3) *Regola rubertina* (modern edn. and facsimile; Peters, 1974).
Gerle, H., *Musica teutsch* (English trans. in *Journal of the Viola da Gamba Society of America*, 6 (1969)).
Le Blanc, H. (1740): *Défense de la basse de viole* (facsimile; Minkoff, Geneva).
Loulié, E. (1700): *Méthode pour apprendre à jouer la violle* (English trans. in *Journal of Viola da Gamba Society of America*, 13 (1976)).
Mace, T. (1676): *Musick's Monument* (facsimile; Centre Nationale de la Recherche Scientifique, Paris, 1958).
Machy, Le Sieur de (1685): Preface to *Pièces de violes* (facsimile; Minkoff, Geneva).
Marais, M. (1686–1725): Avertissements from *Pièces de violes* (5 vols.; Schola Cantorum Basiliensis, Basle).
Mersenne, M. (1639): *Harmonie universelle* (facsimile; Centre Nationale de la Recherche Scientifique, Paris; English trans. Nijhoff).
Ortiz, D. (1553): *Tratado de glosas* (facsimile, Studio per Edizioni Scelte, Florence; Bärenreiter, Kassel).
Playford, J. (1682): *Musick's Recreation on the Viol, Lyra Way* (modern edn.; Heinrichsen, Wilhemshaven)
——(1684): *The Skill of Music* (facsimile; Gregg).
Rognoni, F. (1620): *Selva di varii pasaggi* (facsimile; Forni).
Rousseau, J. (1687): *Traité de la viole* (facsimile; Minkoff, Geneva).
Simpson, C. (1659): *The Division Viol* (Faber, London).
Tillet, —(1732): *Le Parnasse françois* (incl. stories about Marais; Slatkine Reprints, Geneva).

### MODERN TUTORS

Baines, F. (1973): *A Tutor for the Treble, (Tenor, Bass) Viol* (Gamut, Cambridge).
Bishop, M. (1979): *A Method for the Viola da Gamba* (Bishop, Atlanta).
Charbonnier, J.-L. (1979): *La Viole de gambe* (English, French, and German; Heugel, Paris).

Dolmetsch, N. (1953): *12 Lessons for the Viola da Gamba* (with supplements for treble and tenor; Schott, London).
Herman, C. (1990): *Alphabet Soup, a Tablature Primer* (PRB Publications, Albany, Ca.).
Hirsh, O. (1968): *A Viol Tutor* (English, German, and Danish; Hansen, Copenhagen).
Jacquier, P., & Charbonnier, J. L. (1987): *L'Art de Jouer la Basse de Viole* (2 vols.; Heugel, Paris).
Kinney, G. (1979): *A Method for the Viola da Gamba* (Kinney, Wichita, Kansas).
Panofsky, M. (1991): *Bass Viol Technique* (PRB Publications, Albany Ca.).

## BOOKS AND PERIODICALS

Very few books have been written since the eighteenth century specifically about the viol. This list includes the most important ones, and also some recommended reading on related topics.

Bol, H. (1973): *La Basse de viole du temps de Marin Marais et d'Antoine Forqueray* (Bilthoven, Nijmegen).
Brown, H. M. (1976): *Embellishing Sixteenth-century Music* (Oxford University Press).
Dodd, G. (1980–): *Thematic Index of Music for Viols* (5 vols.; Viola da Gamba Society, London).
Dolmetsch, N. (1975): *The Viola da Gamba* (3rd edn.; Heinrichsen, Wilhelmshaven).
Donington, R. (1978): *A Performer's Guide to Baroque Music* (Faber, London).
Einstein, A. (1905), repr. 1972): *Zur deutschen Literatur für Viola da Gamba im 16 und 17 Jahrhundert* (Leipzig).
Hayes, G. R. (1969): *The Viols and Other Bowed Instruments* (Broude Brothers, New York).
Hoover, E. (1977): *A Manual of Viol Care* (Hoover, Saratoga).
Hsu, J. (1981): *A Handbook of French Bass Viol Technique* (Broude Brothers, New York).
Lindley, M. (1984): *Lutes, Viols and Temperaments* (Cambridge University Press, Cambridge).
Monson, C. (1982): *Voices and Viols in England 1600–1650* (Ann Arbor).
Neumann, F. (1982): *Essays on Performance Practice* (Ann Arbor).
Sadie, J. A. (1978): *The Bass Viol in French Chamber Music* (Ann Arbor).
Wilson, J. (ed.; 1959): *Roger North on Music* (Novello, London).
Woodfield, I. (1984): *The Early History of the Viol* (Cambridge University Press, Cambridge).

There are also numerous articles on the viol contained in the periodicals listed below:

*Chelys* (Journal of the Viola da Gamba Society of Great Britain)
*Journal of the Viola da Gamba Society of America*
*Early Music*

and in Sadie, S. (ed.), *The New Grove Dictionary of Music and Musicians* (Macmillan, London, 1980).

# Discography

### ENGLISH CONSORT MUSIC

Byrd, *Consort Music, Songs and Anthems*, Rose Consort of Viols, Naxos 8.550604.
—— *Consort Songs*, The Consort of Musicke, DSLO 596.
Coprario, *3-part Fantasies* (incl. lyra viols), Savall, AS 54.
Dowland, *Lachrimae*, Dowland Consort, BIS 315.
—— *Lachrimae*, The Consort of Musicke, DSLO 517.
—— *Lachrimae or Seaven Teares*, Hesperion XX, CD, AS E8701.
—— *Lachrimae*, The Rose Consort of Viols, CD SAR 55.
—— and Byrd, *Nights Black Bird*, Fretwork, VC7 90795–2.
—— and ——  *Go Nightly Cares*, Fretwork, VC 7 91117–2.
Ferrabosco, Mico, and Anon., *English Consort Music*, The Brownynge Consort (private distribution).
Gibbons, *Fantasies Royales*, Savall/Coin/Casademunt, AS 43.
—— *Cries and Fancies*, Fretwork, VC7 90849–2.
—— *Consort Music, Songs and Anthems*, Rose Consort of Viols, Naxos 8.550603.
—— and Lupo, *Music For Prince Charles*, Parley of Instruments, Hyperion CDA 66395.
Holborne, *Pavans and Galliards*, The Consort of Musicke, DSLO 569.
—— *Various*, The Extempore String Ensemble, E 77027.
—— *Pavans, Galliards, Almaines*, Dowland Consort, BIS CD 469.
——, Byrd, and Gibbons, *Blockflöte und Gambenconsort*, Bruggen, AS 641074.
Jenkins, *Consort Music*, The Consort of Musicke, DSLO 600.
—— *All in a Garden Green*, Rose Consort of Viols., Naxos 8.550687.
Jenkins and Lawes, *17th Century English Music for Viols and Organ*, Les Filles de Sainte Colombe, Ti 95.
Lawes, *Viol Consort Music*, The Consort of Musicke, DSLO 560.
—— *Consort Music and Royal Consorts*, Rose Consort of Viols, Naxos 8.550601
—— *Concord is Conquer'd*, Fretwork, VC 5451472.
—— *Five- and Six-Part Fantasies*, Oberlin Consort of Viols, CMCD-1015.
Lupo, *Consort Music*, The English Fantasy, CD GAU 149.
Purcell, *Fantasies* (complete), London Baroque, ASD 1436311.
—— *Fantasies* (selection), Leonhardt Consort, AQ 641222.
—— *Fantasies for the Viols*, Hesperion XX, Astree E 8536.
—— *Fantasies and In nomines*, Fretwork, VC 545 0622.
Tomkins, *Consort Music for Viols and Voices*, Rose Consort of Viols, Naxos 8.550602

Tye, *Lawdes Deo*, Hesperion XX, Astree E 8708.
Ward, *Madrigals and Fantasias*, The Consort of Musicke, Musica Obscura 070981.
Various, *In nomine*, Fretwork, CD SAR 29.
—— *Elizabethan Christmas Anthems*, The Rose Consort of Viols and Red Byrd, CD-SAR 46.
—— *Born Is The Babe*, The Rose Consort of Viols, Woodm 001–2.
—— *The Field Of Cloth Of Gold*, Musica Antiqua Of London, CD-SAR 51.

### ENGLISH DIVISION/LYRA VIOL

Corkine, Ferrabosco, et al., *Lessons for the Lyra Viol*, Savall, AS 51.
Hume, *The Spirit of Gambo*, Pandolpho, Glossa GCD 920402.
—— *Captaine Hume's Poeticall Music*, Savall, IC 065.
Simpson, Jenkins, Forde, et al., *Music for a Viol*, Kuijken/Kuijken, ACC 8014.
Simpson, Jenkins, and Lawes, *For these Distracted Times*, London Baroque, E 77059.

### ITALIAN AND SPANISH DIVISIONS/ENSEMBLE MUSIC

Bassano, Ortiz, et al., *Virtuoso Ornamentation around 1600*, Savall, IC 165.
Frescobaldi, *Aire e canzone*, Savall, 9502 111.
Ortiz, *Recercadas*, Atrium Musicae HM 2393.
—— *Recercadas*, Savall, Astree E-8717.
Ortiz et al., Music in the Renaissance of Naples, Hesperion XX, ASD 1436291.
Selma, *Musica barocca espanola*, Savall, 9502 088.
Tromboncino, *Frottle* (Renaissance Viols), The Consort of Musicke, DSLO 593.
Various, *L'Art de la Viola Bastarda*, Sophie Watillon, Ligia Lidi 0106020-94.
—— *A Royal Songbook*, Musica Antiqua of London, Naxos 8.553325.
—— *A Florentine Carnival*, London Pro Musica, PCD 825.
—— *Selva de Varii Passaggi*, Maurette, Gallo 30-461.

### GERMAN SOLO MUSIC

Abel, Suite in D minor, Kuijken, Denon CO-75659.
Bach, *Sonatas*, Kuijken, GD 77044
—— *Sonatas*, Savall, CDM 7 631392.
—— *Sonatas*, Dreyfus, Simax PCS 1024.
—— *Sonatas*, Harnoncourt, SAWT 9536—A.
Bach, C. P. E., et al., *Sonatas*, Pandolpho, Tactus TC 71020501.
—— *Pierlot*, RIC 047025.
Schenk et al., *Sonatas*, Trio Sonnerie, GAU 107.

## GERMAN ENSEMBLE MUSIC

Bach, *Actus Tragicus*, Leonhardt Consort, EX6 35558.
Buxtehude, *Cantatas*, Jacobs/Kuijken, ACC 7912.
—— *Trio Sonatas*, Boston Museum Trio, HMB 1089.
—— *Trio Sonatas*, Trio Sonnerie, CD GAU 110.
Buxtehude, *et al.*, The Source of Eternal Light, The Kings Consort, CDE 84126.
Scheidt, Schenk, *et al.*, *German Music for Viols and Harpsichord*, Les Filles de Sainte-Colombe, CMCD–1013.
Telemann, *Paris Quartets*, Linde/van Dael/Savall, ASD 3698.
—— *Trio for Flute & 2 Gambas*, Kuijken, ACC 8019.

## FRENCH SOLO SUITES

Caix d'Hervelois, *Pièces de viole*, Savall, AS 7.
Couperin, *Pièces de viole*, Savall, E 7744.
Forqueray, *Pièces de viole* (complete), Pandolpho, Glossa GCD 920401.
—— *Pièces de Viole* (1st & 2nd Suites), Savall, Astree E7762.
Marais, *1st Book* (selection), Astree E 7769.
—— *2nd Book* (selection), Astree E 7770.
—— *2nd Book* (selection), Dreyfus. Simax PSC 1053.
—— *3rd Book* (selection), Astree, E 8761.
—— *4th Book* (selection), Astree E 7727.
—— *5th Book* (selection) Savall, E 7708.
—— *5th Book* (selection, Kuijken. ACC 78744 D.
—— *Viol Music for the Sun King*, Spectre de la Rose, Naxos 8.553081.
—— *Pièces da Violes*, Cunningham CD GAU 112.
Sainte Colombe, *Duets*, Astree E 7729.
—— and Marais, *The Great Masterworks*, Spectre de la Rose, Naxos 8.550750.

## FRENCH CHAMBER MUSIC

Couperin, *Les Nations*, Hesperion XX, AS 991.
De Caurroy, *Fantasies*, Savall, AS 86.
Marais *La Gamme/La Maresienne*, London Baroque, AM 1105.
—— and Forqueray, *Musique Française*, Kuijken/Leonhardt, HM 20346.
—— and —— *Music in Versailles*, HM 414.
Rameau, *Pièces de clavécin en concert*, Kuijken/Leonhardt, SAWT 9578-B.
—— *Pièces de clavécin en concert*, Boston Museum Trio Ti 28.
—— *Pièces de clavécin en concert*, Trio Sonnerie, VC7 90749–2.

# Index

Abel, C. F. 112
    Sonata in G major 119
    Prelude in D minor 119–20
accompanying recitative 96–7
adjustment of viols 114–5
adult beginners 2
arias 119
arpeggios 119–21
articulation 39–41
    in Bach 116
    in continuo playing 94

Bach, C. P. E. 112, 120
Bach, J. S. 112, 115–19
    *Actus tragicus* 119
    Brandenburg Concerto No. 6: 119
    *St John Passion* 119
    *St Matthew Passion* 119
    Sonata in D major 115–17
    Sonata in G major 114–16
    Sonata in G minor 116–18
    *Trauer ode* 119
bad habits 133, 138
bad sound, causes of 47
Baroque music *see* arias, chamber music, continuo playing, French suites, sonatas
barring *see* fingering
Bassano, G. 98
basso continuo 93
beats 155
Benda, G. 120
*Bergamasca* 104
bow holds 10–12, 80–1
bowing
    back stroke 15–16
    bow speed 48
    changing strokes 17–18
    chords 72–3
    in continuo playing 96
    dotted notes 51–5
    in double stopping 70
    in fantasies 90
    fast notes 48–51
    forward stroke 13–15
    practice 14–15, 17, 129–30
    principles of 12–13
    shape of bow stroke 60
    tensioning of hair 12–13
    triplet bowing 54–5
    uneven bowing 33–4
bows
    choosing 5, 150–2
    cleaning 152
    holding 10–12
    rehairing 153
    Renaissance and Baroque 151
    tightening hair of 10
bridge
    adjustment 5, 144–5
    fitting 145
    straightening 145
Buxtehude, D. 112
Byrd, W. 92

cadences 90, 94, 106
Caix d'Hervelois, L. 122
Campion, T. 93
cantus firmus 83, 91
    *In nomine* 83, 91, 105
    *La Spagna* 83, 105
chamber music 82, 112, 122
children and viols 2
chords
    bowing 72–3
    fingering 71, 99
    in lyra viol 111
    practice 130
    speed of spread 93
clefs
    learning to read 76–7
    for viol music 76
    unfamiliar 78
comma
    Pythagorean 156
    syntonic 156
common faults
    wrist position 15–16, 17
    left hand position 19–20, 29–30
concerts
    listening 134
    planning programme 137
consort music 82–93

consorts
    broken 91
    coaching 136
    concerts and records 134
    keeping your place 135–6
    with other instruments 91–3
    playing in 134–7
    social aspects 136
    tuning 136
consort songs 91–3
continuo playing 93–7
    accompanying voice 96–7
    articulation 94
    harmonic structure 94
    stress 94
    style 93–5
    *see also* bowing, fingering
co-ordination
    practice 130
    on fast notes 50–1
Coprario, G. 83, 106, 108
Corkine, W. 108
Couperin, F. 122
courants 88, 106–7
Corelli, A. 93
crawling 66–7, 113

Dalla Casa, G. 98
dance music 83, 85–90
descanting 105
detached playing 41
diatonic fingering 66, 68, 101
divisions
    chordal passages 98–9
    in dance music 87–8
    duets 103
    English 98–101
    holding down fingers 98
    Italian 97–8
    melodic and harmonic patterns 103
    style 102–3
    *see also* extemporization
Dollé, C. 122, 124
Dolmetsch, A. 1
dotted notes 51–4, 100, 128
double stopping 70–1, 119
Dowland, J.
    *Lachrimae* 91
    Lute songs 92–3
duets 106–7, 120
dynamics 13, 87

early music revival 1

East, M. 106
enharmonics 157–61
ensemble music 82
ensembles, playing in 134–7
Erlebach, P. 120
extemporization 88, 97
    decorating madrigals 105
    descanting 105
    divisions 103–6
    in groups 106
extensions 28–32, 68–9


facsimile 77, 79, 101, 108, 109, 127
fantasies 83, 90–91
Ferrabosco, A. 108
figured bass 96
Finger, G. 112, 120
finger movement
    in fast notes 49–50
    in dotted notes 53
    in slurring 57
fingering
    barring 34–5
    chordal 34–7, 114
    chords 71
    in continuo playing 95–6
    contracted 37
    diatonic 66, 67–8, 101
    in double stopping 70
    holding fingers down 35, 57
    practice 26, 130
Ford, T. 108
Forqueray, J. B. 80, 81, 122, 152
French suites 121–2
French style 123
frets
    adjustment for unequal temperament 163
    for different temperaments 158–9
    moving 150
    splitting 159–60, 162
    tying 149


galliards 85, 88
    cross rhythms in 86
    shape of 87
Ganassi, S. 81, 97, 98, 101, 106, 138
Gibbons, O. 83, 106
Goldsmiths' Company 2
grating sounds 14, 50
ground bass 96, 102, 105

Handel, G. F. 93, 112
  Sonata in A minor 95
  Sonata in C major 120
  Sonata in G minor for recorder 94
  Sonata in G minor for viol 120
Hardy, Thomas 1
harmonic series 155
Hely, B. 106
Heudeline 122
high positions 101–3
Hingeston, J. 106
Holborne, A. 71, 83, 85, 91
  The Funerals 85–6
  Muy Linda 87–8
Hume, T. 3, 108
  I am Falling 112

instrumentation 83
intonation 155–6, 161
  bending notes 163–4

Jenkins, J. 83, 103, 106
  Coranto 88–9
  Ground 105
  Newark Siege 103

Key 26, 27
Kuhnel, A. 112, 120

Lawes, W. 103, 108
learning new pieces 131–2
left-hand position 18–21
  checking 19–20
  for chordal fingering 35
  in extensions 28–30
  first position 22–6
  half position 27–8
legato playing 41
lessons 133–4
Locke, M. 89, 106
  Courante from Suite in D 107
  Sarabande from Suite in D 90
Loulié, E. 7, 42
Lupo, T. 83
Lute songs 91–3
Lyra viol
  bowing 111
  chords 111
  fingering 111–12
  repertoire 108–9

resonance 111
style 107, 111
thump 110
tunings for 110

Mace, T, 8, 17, 46, 135
Machy, Le Sieur de 108, 122
madrigals 91–3, 105
maintenance see viols
Marais, M. 120, 122, 124–5, 128
  Fantasie from Troisieme livre 127
  Ornaments, signs and terms 125
  Prelude in G major 126–7
  Sonnerie de Ste Genevieve 128
  Menuet in A minor 126
  Tableau de l'operation de la taille 128
memory, playing from 133
modern works 82
mordents 124–5

notation 76–80
  facsimile 78–80
  grouping of notes 78
  note lengths 135
  rests 135
  tablature 80, 107, 109
  unfamiliar clefs 78

obbligatos 119
octave leaps 62–4, 96
open strings 22
ornamentation 89, 97
  in German sonatas 113
  in French music 123, 124–6
Ortiz, D. 93, 98, 105, 106
  Doulce Memoire 97
  O felici occhi miei 97
  Recercadas 102

pardessus 122
pavans 83, 85
pegs 5, 44, 145
performing in public 137–8
Playford, J. 108, 110, 111
  Almain from Musick's Recreation on the Viol 108
plucking 86, 128
positions
  first position 22–6
  half position 27–8

practice 129–34
    bowing 14, 129–30
    chords 73–5, 130
    divisions 104
    double stopping 70, 130
    fingering 22–5, 130
    planning of 92, 132
    regularity of 129
    technical difficulties 129
Purcell, H.
    *Music for a while* 96–7
pure intervals 155, 156
*poussez* 13, 123

Rameau, J-P. 122
Renaissance viols 139
repertoire 82, 108–9
resonance
    between strings 21
    and fingering 22, 35
    in lyra viol playing 111
    in new viols 142
    and string crossing 59
rhythm 129
Rognoni 88, 98, 102
    *Selva di varii pasaggi* 88
    *vestiva i colli* 103
rosin 10, 47, 152
Rousseau, J. 7, 104, 123

Sainte-Colombe 122
sarabands 89–90
Schenk, J. 112, 120
    Prelude in D minor 121
shifts and shifting 66–70
    high positions 70, 101
    practice 70, 130
    rules for 68
    on treble 66, 68–9
sight-reading 132
simple pieces 26
Simpson, C. 80, 101, 102–3, 105, 106, 149
    *The Division Viol* 98
    Divisions in E minor 100–2
    Exercises 99
    Prelude in D major 99, 101
    *The Months* 103
    *The Seasons* 103
sitting position 8–9
slurring 55–9, 112, 127
solo music 82
sonatas 112–21

sound post 145
sound quality 5
speed
    building up 131
    in consorts 136
stress
    in continuo playing 94
    in dance music 85–6
    in French music 123, 125
string crossing
    fast 62–5
    jumping strings 62
    octave leaps 62
    practice 130
    and resonance 59
    rules for 37–9
    and shifts 68
    during slurs 58
strings
    sensitivity 5
    types 145–7
    changing 147–8
Sumarte, R.
    *Daphne* 109
summer schools 137, 142

tablature 107, 108–11
Taverner, J. 83
technical faults 134
technique 42, 47
Telemann, G. P. 112
    Sonata in A minor 113
    Sonata in E minor 114, 115
temperaments
    equal 157, 158
    fretting schemes 159
    meantone 157, 158–61
    setting 157
    unequal circular 157, 161–2
    Vallotti 159, 161, 162
    Werckmeister 11, 164
tempering 156–63
thumb 18–21, 68
*tirez* 13, 123
Tomkins, T.
    Pavan a 5 87
tone colour 13
tone quality 18, 46–7
trills 122,
    in Marais 124
    in Simpson 102–3
trios 106
triple time 54–5

tucking 26–7
    dotted notes 54
    in fantasies 90–1
    legato 58–9
tuning
    for beginners 6
    in concerts 138
    in consorts 83–5, 136, 163–4
    by ear 45–6
    electronic meters 44
    importance of 5, 44–6
    with keyboard instruments 164
    with lute 164
tunings 6–7, 110
Tye, C. 83

unbarred music 78

Valotti 159, 161, 162
vibrato 125

*viola bastarda* 98
Viola da Gamba Societies 5
viols
    buying 139–44
    choosing 5
    hiring 5
    holding 7–10
    less common sizes 139–40
    maintenance 144
    in orchestras 138
    second-hand 142
    size 139
Virgiliano, A. 98
voices and viols 82, 96–7

Ward, J. 106
White, W. 106
wind instruments 91
Withy, J. 106
wolf notes 47, 148–9
wrist position 12–16, 17, 19, 48